KEATS

KEATS

Edward Thomas

Introduction by Richard Emeny, Secretary of the
Edward Thomas Fellowship

THE CYDER PRESS
Cheltenham, England

Acknowledgements

The Cyder Press is indebted to Myfanwy Thomas, Edward Thomas's daughter, and the Edward Thomas Fellowship, for permission to reprint, without fee, the first and only edition of *Keats* (T.C. and E.C. Jack, 'The People's Books' series, 1916) in its original form.

This edition first published by The Cyder Press, 1999
Copyright 1999: Introduction: Richard Emeny

ISBN 1 86174 071 9

Published and produced by Cheltenham and Gloucester
College of Higher Education, 1999.

INTRODUCTION

Somerset Maugham, while once visiting the Royal Academy Summer Exhibition, is recounted as standing next to a lady, both of them gazing at a landscape in oils. The lady was, according to Maugham, of a certain type: she undoubtedly came from Cheltenham. Breaking from her admiring gaze, she turned to Maugham and said, ' "A thing of beauty is a joy for ever," I always say.'

'Yes,' responded Maugham, 'Keats said that too, but he only said it once.'

This anecdote is more illustrative of Maugham's wit than of any profound knowledge of Keats, but there was a point: earlier this century Keats was one of the two or three most popular poets in English Literature, much quoted and much admired more than anything for the sensuousness and languor of his verse. The drama of his consumptive death while still young added to the romance. By the time Edward Thomas came to write this ninety-page book tastes were changing, at least among writers if not the general reading public, but he was still a figure of great importance and remains so. The lady's reaction was not untypical of the way in which Keats was thought part of the common currency of the educated public.

If tastes were changing when Thomas wrote *Keats*, they have changed far more since his death at the Battle of Arras on Easter Monday 1917, and it is important to remember that Thomas was almost as close to Keats in time as we are to Thomas. His standpoint was different to ours temporally, and he wrote for an audience with different cultural references, whose background views and accepted norms were far removed from ours.

In some ways this is illustrated by the book itself, now republished for the first time since its appearance in 1916. It was one of a series, *The People's Books*, number 126 to be precise, which was part of that great movement of the late nineteenth and early twentieth centuries towards self-education at an affordable price. A glimpse at the list of titles at the end of the book gives an indication of the breadth of subject matter and the distinction of the authors.

i

The series was simply produced with no frills and each title of a size which could handily be slipped into a pocket. Thomas, apolitical in general, nevertheless had radical sympathies and would have been pleased to help such a worthy movement. An admirer of William Morris, enabling more people to appreciate and enjoy what seemed to him good and important in life would have pleased Thomas.

Whatever his sympathies with the ideals behind the series, Thomas regarded writing *Keats* as yet another chore, another piece of hack-work. He was born on 3rd March 1877 in London but of Welsh background. The quality of his writing had been recognised by his English teacher while he was still a schoolboy, and he was encouraged to persevere in his writing by James Ashcroft Noble, a distinguished man of letters, whose daughter he subsequently married. Since coming down from Oxford in 1899 and deciding to earn his living by writing, his life had been governed by commissioned biographies, criticism and topographical books, for which he had little enthusiasm but which were necessary to support a growing family.

He first mentions *Keats* in a letter to Eleanor Farjeon, dated 'Midsummer 1913': ' ... did I tell you that I had accepted rotten terms to do a rotten little book on Keats?' The terms were just £25. Despite the obvious disgust, the book is far from rotten, Thomas being incapable of slapdash work, and he had indeed thought earlier about writing a book on Keats. In a letter to Gordon Bottomley dated 22nd April 1910, he writes: '... I am still without plans and of course difficulties increase. I have been examining the poems and letters etc. of Keats, Landor, Wordsworth and Donne.' In an earlier letter to Bottomley (27th March 1907), he writes that he is going to see a publisher's reader to discuss a book and is thinking of one on English poetry including Keats. The quotation is witness to the breadth and depth of Thomas's reading: there were few, if any, critics during the Edwardian period who knew so well what they were writing about, whose approval was so sought by aspiring writers, and whose reading was not only wide but perceptive.

In his biography of Maurice Maeterlinck, Thomas makes it clear that he regards himself as an unapologetic 'Elizabethan and Romantics' man, Keats being one of the more important of his early literary heroes. The eighteenth century was less important to him: 'We have in truth long been a little weary of a literature which dealt with nothing that was not discussed at the best houses,' he writes somewhat critically when reviewing *A Later Pepys* in 1904.

Helen Thomas in *As It Was* also witnesses to the importance of Keats and the Romantics during the period when Edward and she were still at school: 'Edward and I were getting much less reserved together, and talked of anything and everything - of poetry a great deal - Keats, Shelley, Coleridge, Wordsworth and Tennyson chiefly, I think - oh and Byron too...'. This importance would not have been unusual in any well-educated person with an interest in English Literature of Thomas's day, but there is in his writing an atmosphere of fellow-feeling which goes beyond an intellectual enthususiasm. It led to his belief that the Romantics should be read in their entirety not just used as mines from which prettry gems could be extracted. 'The complete achievement of the Romantics matters, not just the ore extracted by aesthetes and symbolists,' he comments in *Maurice Maeterlinck*.

One of the changes in English letters which dismayed Thomas was the move from *belles lettres*, to the more professional approach of the 'Schools' of English Literature which came to dominate the rest of the century. Despite his radical sympathies, he was conservative in this at least. Thus on the Milton Memorial Lectures, he lamented that this was '... a cause for regretting that something like taste is not more widely distributed in academic circles.' It is perhaps not surprising that he regarded Coleridge as pre-eminent among critics. Despite this, he was an early exponent of using quotations followed by analysis, not such a common approach at the time as it is now.

There is in this ninety-page book an amount of Keats family history and details of Keats's friends and literary influences such as Spenser and Leigh Hunt, but carefully selected so as to illustrate the poet. There is as well as an examination of Keats's poetry a chapter called simply, '*Character*,' but nothing is irrelevant, and the book feels expansive even though its size means that it cannot really be so. The reason why Thomas adopted this approach may have been partly because he believed the readers of the *People's Books* would find it most useful, but also because, from about 1912 to 1914, he was writing the prose which years later would be published as *The Childhood of Edward Thomas*. He was trying to find his true writing voice during this period - to write as himself. In December 1914 he started writing the poetry for which he is best known now, but there was an intensity of 'working things out' before he started, and his *Keats* was written in parallel with that. Background and biography were to Thomas as illuminating of a poet's work as was formal literary criticism, and this was as true of himself as of Keats. The book can be seen as part of the process of thought by which Thomas himself came to write verse, as well as demonstrating his emerging views on how verse needed to be written.

For all his adult life Thomas had been a critic of poetry: more than one million words of critical journalism are stored in the University of Wales Library in Cardiff. These represent over 1100 reviews of some 1200 books, not all of them poetry, of course, and probably only about two-thirds of his complete criticism. He was nevertheless immersed in poetry and significantly, when he started to write *Keats*, was contemplating writing verse himself. Over a period of years he struggled to find a mode of writing which was appropriate to the twentieth century with its social, economic, political and artistic developments. His prose writing suggests that he foresaw many of these more clearly than most of his contemporaries, and while he wrote about Keats and Jefferies, he was the first to recognise the work of Ezra Pound.

By the time *Keats* was published in March 1916, Thomas had produced much of his poetry, enshrining the poetic beliefs he had developed. *Keats* is therefore important not simply as a useful book about that poet, but as an illustration of the views on verse writing that Thomas had developed so painfully over the years. More obviously, there are echoes of Keats's poetry in some of his poems, notably 'October' and 'Haymaking'. As important was the similarity in temperament between the two men. They both walked and travelled, although Thomas was by far the more active. Keats's great journey to the North of England, Scotland and Northern Ireland evoked a sympathy in Thomas, whose own journeys over England and Wales were a repetitive feature of his life. While the influence of his journeys is to be seen in Thomas's own work, both prose and poetry, he recognised the same in Keats's 'Hyperion' and 'Meg Merrilees'. Keats found he needed to absent himself from Fanny Brawne in order to write. Thomas wrote *Keats* away from home at Selsfield House, East Grinstead, home of his friends, the Locke-Ellises. He too found the distractions and disruptions endemic to home life difficult. 'Between Fanny Brawne and Cap and Bells and the recast of Hyperion, which he called a vision, he divided himself down to the last drop of his life,' he notes.

Two other similarities are worth mentioning. First, Keats's 'negative capability' appears in some of his work, too, in particular in the genius Thomas has for absorbing atmosphere whether of people, places or writing: a few words, a phrase or two and he has transferred to the reader an epitome of his subject. Second, while Keats's consumption was hastening him to his death, so the Great War was beckoning Thomas with similar inevitability. Both were aware of time running out, for although Thomas was over age, and could have remained a map-reading instructor in the army, he volunteered for the Western Front.

Thomas's reflections and years of reading had led him to a belief that a 'common speech' style of poetic diction was the way forward for English verse. It was a theory that he had perfected during long conversations with his friend, the American poet, Robert Frost. Their conclusions have influenced many subsequent poets as dissimilar as Auden, Larkin and Walcott. Consequently, he tends to emphasise the less overtly decorative elements in Keats's work. He selects the simplicity of 'The grass, the thicket, and the fruit-tree wild,' and 'With forest branches and the trodden weed,' because 'they gain from their environment an astonishing beauty.' By contrast, of *Endymion* he says: 'No poem of the same length is so crammed with loveliness and the love of loveliness. No English poem is so impossible to read though with a sense of anything in it before or after the lines immediately under the eye.' This is not only perceptive but the type of truth people find difficult to admit of a 'classic.' It is a far cry from Maugham's Cheltenham lady. What Thomas is indicating is that Keats was still at this period overwhelmed by beauty, by the thrill of life and events, and *had* to tell them all. The later poems, 'Isabella' and 'The Eve of St Agnes', show by contrast a subjugation of the beautiful line to the structure and sense of the whole. Of 'Isabella', which he thought a masterpiece, Thomas wrote: 'It was the first long poem in which Keats put all his luxury, all his pitifulness, in perfect order and combination, and the more effective for being subordinated to the clear telling of a story which was itself sufficiently interesting.' This is a judgement which may now seem unexceptionable, but at the end of the Tennysonian age was less evident.

To escape from the effete element of Keats's languor, Thomas discriminated between languor which enhances life and the merely sickly. He also writes at length and with enthusiasm of Keats's earlier years, of the man's physical and mental activity and agility. The picture that emerges is thus untypical of the Keats of tradition at the time the book was written. That had been too much contaminated by a later and decadent Romanticism. Keats's sensuousness for Thomas goes beyond dreary melancholia to something fresh and life-giving. Thomas admired Keats's pugnacity, as instanced by the often-told story of his fight with the butcher's boy, his gusto, and long evenings spent in vigorous discussion and debate with his friends. Above all it is visible, tangible, audible beauty that Thomas enjoys. Thomas approves of Keats's social concern, and hints that he was probably more closely engaged in supporting radical concerns than had been recognised - or than people had wanted to recognise. Above all, he loves the muscularity of Keats's mind: 'A more earthly poet never lived, though some have been more worldly.'

This is not to say that Thomas does not recognise Keats's morbidity of temperament but he believed it was not the key to the complete man. His analysis of the morbidity and of Keats's character generally seems related to the self-analysis which at the time of writing was leading Thomas to write poetry. That morbidity he found balanced by the directness of Keats's letters, which 'are excelled by none in their direct presentation of the moment's phases of mind and moods and temperament.' In his own poem, 'The Glory', Thomas lamented that 'I cannot bite the day to the core.' Keats had the apparent advantage of being able to do so in abundance.

It is perhaps unwise to draw too many parallels between a biographer's cast of mind and that of his subject, but Thomas always put much of himself into his work. When he was writing about another writer to whom he was much attached - Jefferies or Borrow perhaps - this is especially true and Keats comes into that category. To combine that with objective perception is Thomas's great talent and one of the qualities of this book.

Like Keats, Thomas was brought up in the city, but this did not impel either of them to write. Unlike Thomas, Keats tended to regard the country 'as a picture gallery and pleasure resort.' Keats stresses travel and exercise and good company, but Thomas knew the roadmenders, the farm labourers and the tramps. In the *Daily Chronicle* of 27 August 1901, he said of Keats: 'the best lyrics seem to be the poet's natural speech.' From then until December 1914 Thomas was following this trail and finding his own natural speech with the aid of Keats among others. *Keats* must rank among the best short books about that poet, both as an introduction and as a perceptive and useful exposition. The coincidence of writing the book and beginning to write poetry was a happy one, both Thomas and Keats benefiting.

Richard Emeny

Goathurst, Somerset

KEATS
By EDWARD THOMAS

LONDON: T. C. & E. C. JACK
67 LONG ACRE, W.C., AND EDINBURGH
NEW YORK: DODGE PUBLISHING CO.

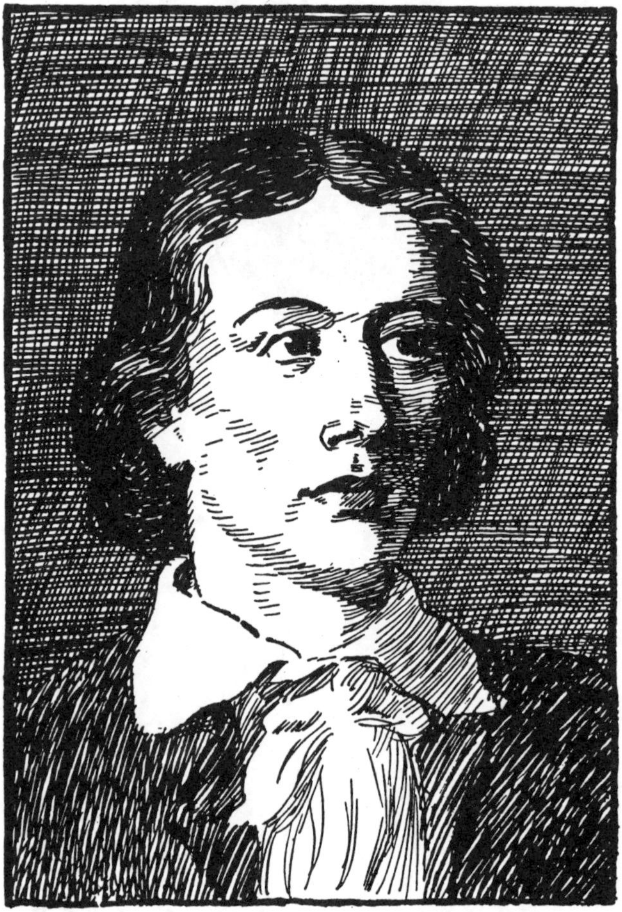

CONTENTS

CHAP.		PAGE
I.	KEATS AND HIS FRIENDS	7
II.	THE FIRST BOOK OF POEMS AND OTHER EARLY POEMS	34
III.	"ENDYMION"	40
IV.	"ISABELLA," "LAMIA," "THE EVE OF ST. AGNES," AND THE ODES	48
V.	"HYPERION," AND THE LAST SONNET	61
VI.	CHARACTER	74
	BIBLIOGRAPHY	91
	INDEX	92

KEATS

CHAPTER I

KEATS AND HIS FRIENDS

WORDSWORTH was a young man at the beginning of the French Revolution, and thought it good to be alive and, above all, to be young. But Keats came into the world twenty-five years later. That glorious time had flared into the Reign of Terror, and the Reign of Terror had died down into the settled government of the Directory. Abroad, England was carrying on war by land and sea, at home suffering from war and its expenses in men and money, from bad harvests and the loss of freedom to speak, to write, and to hold meetings. 1795 was the year of Keats's birth, of the Prince Regent's marriage with Caroline of Brunswick, of the mob at the opening of Parliament crying in the King's ears "No Pitt!", "No Famine!", "No War!" and smashing his coach windows.

Keats came into this world on October 29 or 31, 1795, at a livery stable, "The Swan and Hoop," Finsbury Pavement. His father, Thomas Keats, had been head ostler, but now, having married

Frances Jennings, his master's daughter, was managing the business. John was the first-born, a seven-months' child. The father was a man of "common sense and native respectability," small, keen, brown-haired, hazel-eyed, and said to be from Devon or Cornwall : he was killed by a fall from his horse in 1804, leaving three sons and a daughter, his last born. The mother, tall, shapely, vivacious, talented, and pleasure-loving, resembled John in the face and apparently favoured him and was passionately loved by him. In 1805 she married a second husband named Rawlings, but unhappily : a separation was arranged ; and she settled with her children at Church Street, Edmonton, in the house of her widowed mother. Mr. Jennings had left £200 a year to his widow, to his daughter £50 to revert to her children after her death, and £1000 to be divided amongst them when they came of age. When the mother died of consumption in 1810 the orphans were provided for and put under the care of guardians by their grandmother, who died in 1814 at the age of seventy-eight.

The brothers went to school at Enfield under the Rev. John Clarke. His son, Charles Cowden Clarke, became Keats's friend, though seven years his senior. By him and other contemporaries the boy was remembered as a favourite at school, handsome, vivacious, high-minded, generous, fearless, of an ungovernable temper and fond of fighting, but very tender, with passions of tears and of outrageous laughter. Some of his fights were with George, his next brother, who records that John's temper was always the cause, yet praises him for "the goodness of his heart and the nobleness of his spirit." Towards the end of his schooldays he began to read, at meals and all other respites from lessons, histories, travels, romances, classical dictionaries, and Leigh Hunt's liberal *Examiner:* he set about a translation of the "Æneid" into English prose.

At fifteen, after his mother's death, he was apprenticed by his guardian, Richard Abbey, to an Edmonton surgeon, but continued his translating. Reading Spenser's "Faerie Queene," which Cowden Clarke lent him, awakened his genius. He ramped through the cantos eagerly and luxuriously, tasting to the uttermost that

"Most melodious sound,
Of all that mote delight a daintie eare,
Such as attonce might not on living ground,
Save in this Paradise, be heard elswhere."

The "Imitation of Spenser," afterwards printed in his first book, was probably written during this period, at about the end of 1813. He became a constant versifier, raving that "women, wine, and snuff" shall ever be his "beloved Trinity," or praying for a drug to banish women from his mind, particularly one woman; honouring Spenser, Chatterton, Byron, Apollo; honouring also Hope,

"Sweet Hope, ethereal balm upon me shed,
And wave thy silver pinions o'er my head;

and amusing his friends with doggerel

A quarrel with the surgeon in 1814 sent him to study at St. Thomas's and Guy's Hospitals, and to live at 8 Dean Street, Borough ; then in St. Thomas's Street, then in the Poultry, then in 1817 at 76 Cheapside. His studies qualified him for an appointment as dresser at Guy's Hospital in 1816, and what he did he did well ; but his mind was on poetry, his dexterity in his one operation " seemed a miracle," and he never took up the lancet again. His devotion to poetry, said a fellow student, " prevented his having any other taste or indulging in any vice." But he was thoroughly alive, he enjoyed good health, said another friend, was self-confident, and fond of company and the frivolities of life. Nor did he ignore the politics of the day. Foreign triumph—domestic satiety mingled with discontent—the Corn Laws—the Enclosure Acts—the imprisonment of Leigh Hunt and Cobbett—the enthronement of the First Gentleman of Europe—the rebellion of Byron—made Keats in conversation a radical, republican, and sceptic ; in verse, a lover of Liberty who addressed a sonnet to Kosciusko and another to Peace—

" Let the sweet mountain nymph thy favourite be,
With England's happiness proclaim Europa's Liberty."

It was, however, for the pen, not the sword, nor the sword-pen, that he gave up the lancet. The England of that day could not inspire a young poet, unless it could first banish him, and Keats was by temper unready to play the part which Cobbett played at home in prose, or Shelley and Byron abroad in poetry. In spite of his energy, courage, and independence, he enjoyed and suffered from what he himself called his morbidity of temperament. Those to whom he is known by his poems only, seldom guess at those active qualities unless they have been medicined with the tale of his thrashing the butcher boy that tortured the cat. Such a youth is not suggested even by his earliest verse. In part, this was because he was writing in an atmosphere largely created by Beattie, Mrs. Tighe, and the Rev. Mr. Polwhele. Polwhele's continuation of Beattie's "Minstrel" in the *Poetical Register* for 1810–1811 is stuffed with the panting, thrilling, languor, sweetness, gentleness, deliciousness, faintness, tremulousness, &c., of Keats. What was fun to Polwhele was in the end, however, death to Keats. His morbidity of temperament was inseparably kin to the sensitive passive qualities without which his poetry would have been nothing. I do not mean that his poetry sprang from his morbidity simply, but that both had to do with the brooding intensity of his receptiveness, that they inhabited the same enchanted treasure-caves. Eagerness and joy went with it also. For example, it is clear that old books were to Keats a great delight, and the very great delight of Chapman's *Homer* which he and Cowden Clarke sat over all one night of 1815 in Clerkenwell, is perfectly expressed in the sonnet written by the poet the morning after, at his lodgings in the Borough, and sent to his friend in time for breakfast :

"Much have I travell'd in the realms of gold,
And many goodly states and kingdoms seen;
Round many western islands have I been
Which bards in fealty to Apollo hold.
Oft of one wide expanse had I been told
 That deep-brow'd Homer ruled as his demesne ;
Yet did I never breathe its pure serene
Till I heard Chapman speak out loud and bold:
Then felt I like some watcher of the skies
 When a new planet swims into his ken ;
Or like stout Cortez when with eagle eyes
 He stared at the Pacific—and all his men
Look'd at each other with a wild surmise—
 Silent, upon a peak in Darien."

This sonnet is perhaps the finest, almost certainly the loftiest, of all poems having a book for their subject and confessedly inspired by reading. It does not stand alone. The sonnet beginning

"O golden-tongued Romance with serene lute !
 Fair-plumed Syren ! Queen of far away ! "

was a kind of solemn induction to the solemn music of "King Lear," composed, before re-reading the play, because the greatness of the thing seemed to demand the prologue of a sonnet ; and that other, beginning

"It keeps eternal whisperings around
 Desolate shores . . ."

seems to have owed something to the poet at Carisbrooke being haunted by the passage from "King Lear"—"Do you not hear the sea ? " He wrote a sonnet on the blank space of a page at the end of

Chaucer's "The Floure and the Lefe," comparing the tale to a little copse—

"The honied lines so freshly interlace."

Leigh Hunt's "Story of Rimini" moved him to the sonnet :

"Who loves to peer up at the morning sun,
With half-shut eyes and comfortable cheek,
Let him, with this sweet tale, full often seek
For meadows where the little rivers run. . . ."

The fifth canto of Dante's "Inferno" gave him the dream, "one of the most delightful enjoyments I ever had in my life," which is recorded in the sonnet beginning

"As Hermes once took to his feathers light."

The three great things of the age, as it seemed to Keats, were Wordsworth's "Excursion," B. R. Haydon's pictures, and Hazlitt's depth of taste. His letters and early poems overflow with his joy in books, either devoured with friends—

"The grand, the sweet, the terse, the free, the fine:
What swell'd with pathos, and what right divine:
Spenserian vowels that elope with ease,
And float along like birds o'er summer seas:
Miltonian storms, and more, Miltonian tenderness,
Michael in arms, and more, meek Eve's fair slenderness,"

or brooded on alone in the "tall woods with high romances blent." For after giving up the lancet he lived very much on books, and with books, in passionate intimacy. When he writes a poem to a poet or stops in "Endymion" to apologise to an old poet or old tale, it is with a friendliness lacking in Milton's reference to Homer, or Wordsworth's to Milton, or Tennyson's to Wordsworth. Books had for him an intense reality, and sometimes gave him an "overpowering idea" of the dead poets. He could not exist without poetry. "Whenever you write," he said to Reynolds, "say a word or two on some passage in Shakespeare that may have come rather new to you" : he himself had never found so many beauties in the sonnets as during his stay at Burford Bridge in November 1817. In another place he ranks passages of Shakespeare with sun, moon, and stars, among "things real," as distinguished from "things semi-real" and "nothings." The notes on the margin of his copy of Shakespeare admit us to a share of his delight. For example, opposite some lines in the first scene of the second act of "A Midsummer Night's Dream" he comments that "There is something exquisitely rich and luxurious in Titania's saying 'Since the middle Summer's Spring,' as if bowers were not exuberant and covert enough for fairy sports until the second sprouting— which is surely the most bounteous overwhelming of all Nature's goodness. . . . O Shakespeare, thy ways are but just searchable! The thing is a piece of profound verdure." Truthfully did he say that, since he could read and " perhaps understand Shakespeare to his depths," he had reason to be content. For another example from this marginalia, take that opposite the lines from Book I of "Paradise Lost":

"Or have ye chosen that place
After the toil of battle to repose
Your wearied virtue, for the ease you find
To slumber here, as in the vales of Heaven?"

He comments: "There is a cool pleasure in the very sound of vale. The English word is of the happiest chance. Milton has put vales in heaven and hell with the very utter affection and yearning of a great poet." Another note shows how he allowed the poetry to suck him down into its caves and crevices. The passage quoted is where Satan enters the serpent,

"but his sleep
Disturbed not, waiting close the approach of morn."

"Whose spirit," asks Keats, "does not ache at the smothering and confinement—the unwilling stillness —the *waiting close?* Whose head is not dizzy at the possible speculations of Satan in the serpent prison? No passage of poetry can ever give a greater pain of suffocation."

With a very different hearty admiration he copies out a winged smiting passage from Hazlitt and sends it to his brother and sister-in-law, together with a description of himself sitting late, "with one foot rather askew upon the rug and the other with the heel a little elevated from the carpet"—writing on a copy of "The Maid's Tragedy" which he has been reading since tea with great pleasure; and alongside of the Beaumont and Fletcher on the table, are two volumes of Chaucer and a new work of Tom Moore's

called "Tom Cribb's Memorial to Congress"—
"nothing in it," he tells them.

His reading was chiefly in English literature, and particularly in what belonged to the ages before the Puritan revolution, the ages of Chaucer and of Shakespeare, Spenser, Milton, and the dramatists. Next to poetry, he seems to have loved Burton's *Anatomy of Melancholy* among older books. Of his contemporaries, Leigh Hunt, Wordsworth, Byron, and Hazlitt, though not all the same time, were his gods, well on this side of idolatry. Hazlitt's already mentioned invective, and a lusty March mood in 1819, drove him to the pronouncement that he admired Hazlitt; that he did not admire Leigh Hunt, Tom Moore, Bob Southey, and Mr. Rogers, and liked half of Wordsworth and none of Crabbe. His admiration for Chatterton was very great: later in that same year, when he was in revolt against the influence of Milton on his "Hyperion," he declared that the purest English, " or what ought to be the purest," was Chatterton's; he preferred the "northern" native music of it to Milton's. The poetry of Greece and Italy he read in translations, though he began late to make himself as good an Italian scholar as he was a French one, by reading Ariosto, and to get " complete in Latin." The one book which he carried in his northern walking tour was Cary's *Dante*.

English literature, English poetry the Muse of his native land, that " first-born on the mountains," as he calls her, was a main part of what England meant for

Keats. Nature and poetry joined influences, as they did in the origin of the sonnet,

> "It keeps eternal whisperings around
> Desolate shores . . ."

"I like, I love England—I like its living men—give me a long brown plain for my money, so that I may meet with some of Edmund Ironside's descendants": so he wrote from Teignmouth in 1818. And, his short life and short purse notwithstanding, he travelled and sojourned in many parts of this island, almost always in the company of friends. Half of his life he dwelt in the rustic outskirts of London, at Enfield, Edmonton, or Hampstead. He spent many weeks at Teignmouth, at Carisbrooke and Shanklin, at Margate, at Winchester, at Oxford, at Bedhampton and Chichester, at Burford Bridge. When he was twenty-two, with his friend Charles Armitage Brown, he started in June and walked from Lancaster, past Rydal, Ambleside, and Keswick, round Derwentwater, through Keswick, Ireby, and Wigton, to Carlisle. There they took coach to Dumfries; and then on foot again traversed Galloway to the sea, to Kirkcudbright and Portpatrick, whence they took ship to Ireland and got as far as Belfast. Returning to Portpatrick they visited Kirk Alloway, Ayr, Glasgow, Dumbarton, Loch Fyne, Inverary, Loch Awe, and Oban. They crossed to Mull and Staffa and Fingal's Cave. From Oban they went on to Fort William, climbed Ben Nevis, and in early August reached Inverness. A sore throat drove the poet home by sea

B

from Cromarty. The huge and the little things—the hills and great waters of the north, the noises of unseen shepherds in the high mists, the cold air that gives "that same elevation which a cold bath gives one," the glorious mountain evening that left him "worldly enough" to wish for "a fleet of chivalry Barges, Trumpets, and Banners just to die away" before him along the lake into "that blue place among the mountains"—the "wood-alleys, and copses, and quick freshes" of the Isle of Wight, all delighted him. When he rested he made verses. We still have his "lines written in the Highlands after a visit to Burns's country," a sonnet written on the top of Ben Nevis, a sonnet to Ailsa Craig:

"Hearken, thou craggy ocean pyramid!
   Give answer from thy voice, the sea-fowls' screams!
   When were thy shoulders mantled in huge streams?
When, from the sun, was thy broad forehead hid?
How long is't since the mighty power bid
   Thee heave to airy sleep from fathom dreams?
   Sleep in the lap of thunder or sunbeams,
Or when grey clouds are thy cold coverlid.
Thou answer'st not; for thou art dead asleep;
   Thy life is but two dead eternities—
The last in air, the former in the deep;
   First with the whales, last with the eagle-skies—
Drown'd wast thou till an earthquake made thee steep,
   Another cannot wake thy giant size."

His early poems are full of his delight, fresh from the meadows, brooks, and copses, in pretty things, in blossoms, birds, fishes, translated into rhyming words pretty as themselves. Choosing to work

among them, he stole their sweetness for his pages,
and as he sat down to write, could not but tell us
that he began his " Endymion " :

> "Now while I cannot hear the city's din;
> Now while the early budders are just new,
> And run in mazes of the youngest hue
> About old forests; while the willow trails
> Its delicate amber; and the dairy pails
> Bring home increase of milk . . ."

he did not hide his hope :

> " O may no wintry season, bare and hoary,
> See it half-finished : but let Autumn bold,
> With universal tinge of sober gold,
> Be all about me while I make an end."

Nature's loveliness aided the delicacy and the sublimity of his work, his journeyings and sojournings were fertile to the end. Not only does " old Skiddaw " give a simile to " Endymion," but the Scottish days, particularly those at Glenside, Ben Nevis, and Fingal's Cave, are recalled by several passages of " Hyperion," such as the description of Thea conducting Saturn through aged boughs that yielded like

> " the mist
> Which eagles cleave, upmounting from their nest;"

the place where the ruined Titans mourned but could not be heard

> " for the solemn roar
> Of thunderous waterfalls and torrents hoarse,
> Pouring a constant bulk, uncertain where.
> Crag jutting forth to crag, and rocks that seemed
> Ever as if just rising from a sleep,
> Forehead to forehead held their monstrous horns;"

and the picture of Saturn :

> " whose hoary locks
> Shone like the bubbling foam about a keel
> When the prow sweeps into a midnight cove."

In those friendly poetic epistles of his youth this natural beauty was just one of the pleasures of life, and when he longed for ten years to overwhelm himself in poesy, the first were to be spent, as he was then living, in the realm of " Flora and old Pan," where he could

> " sleep in the grass,
> Feed upon apples red, and strawberries,
> And choose each pleasure that his fancy sees. . . ."

A more earthly poet never lived, though some have been more worldly. Thinking happily over the yesterday of pleasure, and the sleepless night following of images and memories from which he rose " refreshed and glad, and gay," he scribbled on, while

> " lovely airs
> Are fluttering round the room like doves in pairs."

But it would be deceptive to omit that in another and later mood he called the elements " no mean comforters " :

" The open sky sits on our senses like a sapphire crown ; the air is our robe of state ; the earth is our throne, and the sea a mighty minstrel playing before it . . ."

Keats must always share his pleasure either by letter or poem. In those days, when he was twenty-two, he seems hardly to have written a poem unconnected with one or more of his friends. It would be addressed to them; its source or matter was something done or said in their company; or it was composed in a friendly competition, as the sonnet on the Grasshopper was with Leigh Hunt, that on the Nile with Shelley. To his friend Reynolds he promised, during their separations, to send a lyric with every letter. No poet has spent a greater part of his apprenticeship in this social, pedestrian style.

Chief among his friends were his two brothers, George and Tom, two and four years younger than himself; and his sister Fanny, eight years younger. His love for his brothers, said Keats himself, before he had met Fanny Brawne, was an affection "passing the love of women." They were perfectly free and intimate together. George, with his sound temperament, bore with the poet, relieved, cheered, and idolised him to the end, whether they were neighbours or separated as they were after 1818 by the Atlantic. Tom, who died of consumption at the end of 1818, understood his brother better than any man living : so said George. With his young sister, living at her guardian's, Keats was sometimes tenderly condescending to her "little wants and enjoyments," her "little troubles," sometimes open in a grave mood or in the playfulness that ran on thus in April 1819 : " O there is nothing like fine weather, and health, and books, and a fine country, and a contented mind, and a diligent habit of reading and thinking, and an amulet against ennui—and, please heaven, a little claret wine cool out of a cellar a mile deep—with a few or a good many ratafia cakes—a rocky basin to bathe in, a strawberry bed to say your prayers to Flora in, a pad nag to go you ten miles or so ; two or three sensible people to chat with ; two or three spiteful folks to spar with ; two or three odd fishes to laugh at ; and two or three numskulls to argue with—instead of using dumb-bells on a rainy day—

> "Two or three Posies
> With two or three simples—
> Two or three Noses
> With two or three pimples—
> Two or three wise men
> And two or three ninnys—
> Two or three purses
> And two or three guineas. . . ."

Serious poems he inscribed to both brothers, and he copied many poems fresh from his brain into letters to them and his sister-in-law, George's wife. What George said of John and himself is as true of all four, that they were more attached than brothers and sisters " ever are." Writing to George and his wife in America a little before Tom's death, the poet said : " I have Fanny and I have you—three people whose happiness to me is sacred—and it does annul that selfish sorrow which I should otherwise fall into, living as I do with poor Tom who looks upon me as his only comfort—the tears will come into your eyes—let them and embrace each other—thank heaven for what happiness you have, and after thinking a moment or two that you suffer in common with all.

Mankind hold it not a sin to regain your cheerfulness."

The poet shared all his literary life, plans, and achievements with his brothers. Most of his other friends were themselves connected with literature, Leigh Hunt being the first and most conspicuous of them, and, since he gave Keats many friends and a model for his early poetry, the most influential. In 1815, at the end of his two years' imprisonment for libelling the Regent, Leigh Hunt had been saluted by a sonnet from Keats. Eleven years older than the poet, he was a man already notable for his luscious verses and his political courage. In private life he was a Bohemian, a radical in politics, in literature the herald of a " freer spirit of versification." A poet with a strong taint of what was not inaccurately labelled cockneyism, a graceful firesider in prose, a cheerful and loyal friend. His poetry, the friendly cottage with books and busts, music and " elegant chat," his combination of

"The rose, the violet, and the spring,
The social smile, the chain for Freedom's sake,"

seemed to Keats to make up for the lack of Grecian glory and beauty and of the

"Crowd of nymphs soft-voiced, and young, and gay
In woven baskets bringing ears of corn,
Roses and pinks, and violets, to adorn
The shrine of Flora in her early May."

His " Story of Rimini," published just before their first meeting in 1816, abounded in sweet pictures of choice and gallant things, exactly to Keats's taste; and Keats, in fact, set about writing lines barely distinguishable from such a model as

> " A land of trees,—which reaching round about
> In shady blessing stretch'd their old arms out ;
> With spots of sunny openings, and with nooks
> To lie and read in, sloping into brooks,
> Where at her drink you startled the slim deer,
> Retreating lightly with a lovely fear.
> And all about, the birds kept leafy house,
> And sung and darted in and out the boughs ;
> And all about a lovely sky of blue
> Clearly was felt, or down the leaves laugh'd through ;
> And here and there, in every part, were seats,
> Some in the open walks, some in retreats,—
> With bow'ring leaves o'erhead, to which the eye
> Look'd up half sweetly and half awfully,—
> Places of nestling green for poets made. . . ."

Keats quoted this last line at the head of " I stood tiptoe," wrote sonnets to Hunt, one dedicating "Endymion" to him, crowned him with ivy, and earned his " Bravo, Keats ! " for a sonnet written at his own table in competition with himself. They were attacked together by Hunt's political enemies, the Scotch reviewers, as cockney poets ; and, in fact, Keats had taken as readily to the worse as to the better vein in Hunt. In a year or two Keats had too much of him, had misunderstandings with him, sickened of him, classed him with Tom Moore, but never, alive or dead, had from him anything but praise and loyalty, and in his last year of life was for a time an invalid under Hunt's roof. Through

Hunt, Keats met the painter of the sublime, of "The Entry of Christ into Jerusalem" and "Xenophon and the Ten Thousand seeing the Sea," B. R. Haydon, who was ten years older than the poet. He was an exuberant man of top-heavy sublime conceptions, and he made Keats see and feel, as he himself did, far more than he ever confided in a legitimate manner to canvas. Keats lived and thrived on admiration for "this glorious Haydon," one of his "great spirits" who "now on earth are sojourning." Through Haydon, who had caused England to buy the Elgin Marbles, Keats came to know these and other truly sublime things. It was at Haydon's that Mungo Park, Landseer, Keats, Wordsworth, and Lamb were dining when Lamb took a lamp to explore the bumps of the inept Commissioner of Stamps. Wordsworth had also written sonnets to Haydon. The man had a divine flowing energy and helped to unlock what Keats possessed of it. Keats lent him money but the return of it was more difficult to obtain than the eloquence of undying gratitude: "Lawk! Molly there's been such doings," said Keats, when Haydon and Hunt were quarrelling. The painter of the sublime lived on, and did not fully act on his contempt for this petty and neglectful world until 1846, when he shot himself dead.

These were great men. A more complete friend was John Hamilton Reynolds. He was a year younger than Keats—an insurance clerk—a poet who had dedicated volumes to Byron and Haydon—a wit, collaborator with Hood in "Odes and Addresses to Eminent Persons," and a friend who had set his heart on having Keats recognised; himself, he said, content with his friend's fame and in being his " steady and affectionate friend." Some of Keats's best letters were to Reynolds and his sisters. When Keats was in London they met frequently. The two were happy confident equals in all moods, as might be guessed from Keats's epistle to Reynolds, beginning with " Junius Brutus, pretty well so-so," and the like, ending with his vision of Nature's " eternal fierce destruction "—

"The Shark at savage prey,—the Hawk at pounce,—
The gentle Robin, like a Pard or Ounce,
Ravening a worm. . . ."

To Reynolds's sonnet on dark eyes, Keats sent a reply in praise of blue. The two planned a set of tales from Boccaccio, Reynolds producing two in "The Garden of Florence," Keats his " Isabella or the Pot of Basil." When Reynolds forestalled Wordsworth with a merry " antenatal " *Peter Bell* in 1819, Keats reviewed the "false Florimel," being one part amused by its humour and " three parts sorry " that Wordsworth should be so baited. The two exchanged verses. In one letter of January 1818—written too, when they were not far apart and were soon to meet—Keats copied out for Reynolds, if he did not compose on the spur of the moment, for he could not " write sense that sunshiny morning," his " O blush not so ! " and " Hence Burgundy, Claret, and Port," and moreover his latest written sonnet,

" When I have fears that I may cease to be . . ."

A few days later he was writing to thank his friend for a "dish of filberts," that is to say, for the "Robin Hood" sonnets which begot his own "Honour to bold Robin Hood." Reynolds's sonnets are equal to all but the very best written by Keats in the same vein, especially the one beginning

"The trees in Sherwood forest are old and good,"

and ending

"Go there with Summer, and with evening,—go
In the soft shadows like some wandering man,—
And thou shalt far amid the forest know
The archer men in green, with belt and bow,
Feasting on pheasant, river-fowl, and swan,
With Robin at their head, and Marian "—

and the last of the three :

" With coat of Lincoln green and mantle too,
And horn of ivory mouth, and buckle bright,
And arrows wing'd with peacock feathers light,
And trusty bow well gather'd of the yew—
Stands Robin Hood :—and near, with eyes of blue
Shining through dark hair, like the stars of night,
And habited in pretty forest plight—
His green-wood beauty sits, young as the dew.
Oh gentle-tressed girl ! Maid Marian !
Are thine eyes bent upon the gallant game
That stray in the merry Sherwood : thy sweet fame
Can never, never die. And thou, high man,
Would we might pledge thee with thy silver Can
Of Rhenish, in the woods of Nottingham ! "

Keats responded not only with thanks and a genial hearty plea *for* Reynolds's sonnets, the old Poets, and Robin Hood, and *against* Wordsworth's tamest stuff and the moderns in general, but with his own forest-flavoured verses on Robin Hood and that dainty pie fetched from " the Mermaid in the Zodiac "—

> "Souls of Poets dead and gone
> What Elysium have ye known,
> Happy field or mossy cavern,
> Fairer than the Mermaid Tavern ? . . ."

Reynolds was a merry man. His sonnet on the Nonpareil, Jack Randall—

"Good with both hands, and only ten stone four"—

is of all pugilistic verse the most worth remembering. But he took to the law, and Keats pictures him having French lessons with this end, at half-crown a lesson —" the man sells his lessons so cheap he must have stolen 'em."

Reynolds was " the playfullest " of Keats's three witty friends; James Rice being the " wisest," and one Richards " the out-o'-the-wayest." Reynolds, said Keats, was Tom Cribean, Rice Swiftean, Richards Shandean : " and yet these three eans are not three eans but one ean." They were for the cheerfullest years of Keats's youth a close set of friends, who met to talk, to play cards, to drink claret, to imitate a band, until dawn of day. Rice, " dear generous, noble, James Rice," an unsoliciting solicitor, a man who had all things but health, " the best, and in his quaint way one of the wittiest and wisest men," became known to Keats through Reynolds, as did Charles Wentworth Dilke, and Charles Armitage Brown also, friends who were six and nine years, respectively, older than the poet. Dilke and Brown were next-door neighbours at Wentworth Place, Hampstead. Keats boarded for long periods with Brown. There he worked at "Hyperion," and wrote the "Ode to a Nightingale," and some of his other odes and best short poems; and there spent much of his last year, sick to death and occupied with "Cap and Bells." Brown and the poet stayed at Shanklin together, collaborating at "Otho the Great," and were the guests of some relatives of Dilke's at Chichester and Bedhampton. Brown, a canny and jovial man, a retired Russia-merchant, was thus ironically painted by Keats:

"The slang of cities in no wise he knew,
Tipping the wink to him was heathen Greek;
He sipp'd no 'olden Tom' or 'ruin blue,'
Or Nantz, or cherry-brandy drank full meek
By many a damsel brave, and rouge of cheek;
Nor did he know the aged watchman's beat,
Nor in obscured purlieus would he seek
For curled Jewesses, with ankles neat,
Who, as they walk abroad, make tinkling with their feet."

He was afterwards a friend of Edward Trelawny and a Shakesperean critic; he planned to edit the works of Keats but only wrote a memoir. Dilke was first a civil servant, afterwards a critic, and for many years editor and manager of the *Athenæum*.

Among other friends was Richard Woodhouse, a young barrister who took copies of Keats's letters and manuscript poems and bequeathed them to modern editors. And there was Joseph Severn, the artist, two years older than Keats, and remembered for his portraits of the poet and his companionship during the voyage to Italy and the last weeks at Rome : and Benjamin Bailey an undergraduate of Magdalen College, Oxford, with whom Keats stayed in 1817, working at "Endymion," talking of Chatterton and Wordsworth, boating and walking, visiting Stratford-on-Avon. It was in a letter to Bailey that Keats said he was certain of nothing but " the holiness of the Heart's affections, and the truth of imagination." The poet was ever an eager and loyal friend ; he drew to himself men of matchable temper ; and he said once that he did not know a person " to whom so many purse-strings would fly open " as to him, if he could take advantage of them, which he could not do, because none of the owners was rich. His acquaintances were many. Through Hunt he saw Shelley several times. In a lane at Highgate he met his Guy's Hospital demonstrator and with him Coleridge. Arriving an hour too late at one of Hazlitt's lectures in 1818, he was pounced on by Hazlitt, Charles Wells (not yet the author of "Joseph and His Brethren "), the Landseers, and others. Dining with Horace Smith and his brothers, witty men, convinced him " how superior humour is to wit, in respect of enjoyment."

Whether they are to be called friends or acquaintances, several women of his own age, including Reynolds's sisters, were on good terms with Keats up to the time when he met Fanny Brawne. His letters to these women suggest a comradeship, not deep, but frank and free, and almost equal, for which parallels are not easily found outside our own age. If there was condescension in his kindness towards his young sister it was not blind : he wrote to her, as Dr. A. C. Bradley says, as " an equal who happened to be her senior." His sister-in-law, the "nymph of the downward smile and sidelong glance," whose maiden name was Georgiana Wylie, he loved like a brother, with an additional sentiment due to his having learnt from her that " to see an entirely disinterested girl quite happy is the most pleasant and extraordinary thing in the world." His tenderness and admiration for her were " as great and more chaste " than he could have for any other woman ; so he told her himself. Yet at one time he came to the verge of being in love with her and had written stanzas proposing to sit at her feet in the evening glades,

"While my story of Love I enraptur'd repeat."

There was another woman whom he would have been content to know, as he did Georgiana, for her " mind and friendship alone." Once or twice he met her, and once accompanied her home to 34 Gloucester Street, Queen Square. He had " warmed to her " and kissed her, yet had " no libidinous thought about her." A " lady seen for a few moments at Vauxhall " had snared him by the ungloving of her hand and thrived in his memory so as to inspire a sonnet five years later. For the generality of women, their beauty, as did that of Miss Cox, Reynolds's cousin—

a " Charmian " with " a rich eastern look " whose entrance produced " an impression the same as the Beauty of a Leopardess "—sometimes haunted and fevered him, and he had to make resolutions, as in July 1818, to conquer his passions better than he had done. More often, he was impatient with them —" Is it," he asked, " because they fall far beneath my boyish imagination ? "—unless he met them outside a drawing-room ; then he could either adore the " milk-white lamb that bleats for man's protection," or be casually gallant, as to the " little barmaids " in Devon. Thus he came to class women in his books " with roses and sweetmeats." He never thought to marry. The roaring of the wind, he said, was his wife, and the stars through the windowpane his children. Even after he had fallen in love with Fanny Brawne he thought that a man in love cut " the sorriest figure in the world " ; nothing so struck him with a sense of the ridiculous as love. And at one time, as he shows in a note to the *Anatomy of Melancholy*, thought of the relationship between the love of God and the love of women filled him with disgust. Yet he expressed light love with a freshness and a lack of cynicism very rare in those or any other days, when he wrote the lines beginning

> " Unfelt, unheard, unseen,
> I've left my little queen,
> Her languid arms in silver slumber lying :
> Ah ! through their nestling touch,
> Who—who could tell how much
> There is for madness—cruel or complying ? "

Terribly did he squander his knowledge in "Endymion" by mixing it with fancies and multiplying it into

"half awake
I sought for her smooth arms and lips, to slake
My greedy thirst with nectarous camel-draughts;"

and

"There she lay,
Sweet as a musk-rose upon new made hay;
With all her limbs on tremble, and her eyes
Shut softly up alive . . ."

and

"One gentle squeeze,
Warm as a dove's nest among summer trees,
And warm with dew at ooze from living blood."

Before intimacy ripened with the one woman whom he loved he was struck by mortal sickness.

CHAPTER II

THE FIRST BOOK OF POEMS AND OTHER EARLY POEMS

KEATS began to write poetry with the inevitable imitation of the forms and tones which he admired in his contemporaries and the older poets, but with an exceptional fidelity to his own thought, feeling, and observation. Of his friends, his personal tastes, his admirations and aspirations, his first book, published in 1817, when he was twenty-one, tells quite directly far more than any book of a contemporary. Very few pieces are mere exercises in sentiment. In the great majority he is curiously and deliberately true to the facts of outward form and inward feeling. The poem, for example, addressed to the girl who was afterwards his sister-in-law, while indulging in the fancy

" Hadst thou lived when chivalry
Lifted up her lance on high . . ."

is also a detailed flattery of what the poet admired in her, from the eyelashes that were

" Like the feathers from a crow
Fallen on a bed of snow,"

to the neat ankles, and especially

> "Those beauties, scarce discerned
> Kept with such sweet privacy,
> That they seldom meet the eye
> Of the little loves that fly
> Round about with eager pry.
> Saving when with freshening lave,
> Thou dipp'st them in the taintless wave,
> Like twin water-lilies born
> In the coolness of the morn."

And so, in other classes of poems, he reveals

> "The brain new-stuffed, in youth, with triumphs gay
> Of old romance."

But not only this, the things seen in books and Nature are also revealed, often together, as when he pictures the nymphs

> "wiping
> Cherishingly Diana's timorous limbs"

and her mantle at the bath's edge moving

> "With the subsiding crystal : as when ocean
> Heaves calmly its broad swelling smoothness o'er
> Its rocky marge, and balances once more
> The patient weeds, that now unshent by foam
> Feel all about their undulating home."

Whole sonnets are given to his extreme delight in Chapman's *Homer* and the Elgin Marbles. He glances at his social pleasures, at his dislikes, as for

> "The scarlet coats that pester human kind."

Deepest of all, he went into his own poetic beliefs, his

scorn for the age of Pope, his acknowledgment of the "fairer season" that had come—

"Fine sounds are floating wild about the earth;"

his enjoyment of visible, tangible, audible, beauty; his forward looking towards the time when he must bear the "burden and the mystery of all this unintelligible world," and perhaps help

"To soothe the cares, and lift the thoughts of man,"

or be one of the poet kings

"Who simply tell the most heart-easing things;"

his awe and fear of the task.

Therefore hardly a page of this imperfect book lacks some substantial excuse for pleasure as well as interest. The very quality which made an approach to perfection seldom possible is what also gave them substance, *i.e.* Keats's fidelity to the observation or feeling of the hour. His early poems are an intimate poetic journal. The verse form was the complimentary crown placed, out of gratitude, upon the pleasures of his life. That he really hoped for poetry to spring direct from these pleasures is shown by the sonnet " on leaving some friends at an early hour " :

" Give me a golden pen, and let me lean
   On heap'd up flowers, in regions clear, and far ;
   Bring me a tablet whiter than a star,
  Or hand of hymning angel, when 'tis seen
  The silver strings of heavenly harp atween :
   And let there glide by many a pearly car,
   Pink robes, and wavy hair, and diamond jar [? tiar]
  And half discovered wings, and glances keen.

> The while let music wander round my ears
> And as it reaches each delicious ending,
> Let me write down a line of glorious tone,
> And full of many wonders of the spheres :
> For what a height my spirit is contending !
> 'Tis not content so soon to be alone."

A verse beginning

> "I had a dove and the sweet dove died"

he actually wrote " to some music as it was playing " late in 1818 ; and we know that he wrote sonnets in Burns's cottage, on Ben Nevis, and in sight of Ailsa Craig, straight from his first shock of emotion. And these last two and several other sonnets, like that on Chapman's *Homer* and the second of the two on the Elgin Marbles, prove that the brief disciplinary form of the sonnet, with an emotion strong enough to crush mere fancy and observation, could combine rapidly to fine though sometimes broken results. But more often than not, at the beginning, he was content with " a line of glorious tone," with close and lovely details like

> "The sweet buds which with a modest pride
> Pull droopingly, in slanting curve aside,
> Their scanty-leaved, and finely tapering stems,
> Had not yet lost their starry diadems
> Caught from the early sobbing of the morn."

They were observed as he walked, or even as he lay writing, for he says once :

> "These things I thought
> While, in my face, the freshest breeze I caught.
> E'en now I am pillow'd on a bed of flowers."

The beauty of Nature immediately suggested the beauty of poetry and the translation of one into the other : as he says,

"No sooner had I stepped into these pleasures,
Than I began to think of rhymes and measures.
The air that floated by me seem'd to say,
'Write! thou wilt never have a better day.'
And so I did."

Perhaps with a misgiving that many of these lovely things were not sufficiently made his own he sowed very thick among them words expressive of his own delight in them—words like "soft," "tender," "pleasant," "sweet," "tremulous," "tremble," "nestle," "luxury," "languishment," "trance."

Catalogues of beautiful objects came to him easily. It was all very well to give his brother a catalogue of things seen from the coach as he rode to Southampton—" dusty Hedges—sometimes Ponds—then nothing—then a little wood with trees look you like Launce's Sister 'as white as a Lily and as small as a Wand '—then came houses which died away into a few straggling Barns—then came hedge trees aforesaid again. As the lamplight crept along the following things were discovered—'long heath broom furze'—Hurdles here and there half a mile—Park palings when the windows of a House were discovered by reflection—one nymph of fountain—N.B. *Stone* [? the nymph was stone]—lopped trees—cow ruminating—ditto donkey—Man and Woman going gingerly along—William seeing his Sisters over the heath—John waiting with a Lanthorn for his Mistress—Barber's Pole—Doctor's Shop : " it was not so well to attempt ramming such things into verse. He had not yet learned, or set himself the lesson, that a gradual ripening, a natural overflowing, was perhaps necessary to poetry.

It was therefore to be expected that a disconnected rhyming of his pleasures and hopes should gain attention only from his friends and his natural kindred. To like, or to be capable of, watching minnow and goldfinch is not obligatory to a lover of poetry, but it is almost so to one who is to enjoy many of these poems. By writing them Keats discovered his power to fit "aptest words to things" —if not its inadequacy for poetry—and proved himself, and began to train himself, to be, though a lover of the moon, a most sublunary poet, earthly, substantial, and precise, a man, but for his intensity, singularly like his fellow-men, and more like them than any other great poet since Shakespeare.

CHAPTER III

"ENDYMION"

Two months after the "Poems" were published, Keats began to write "Endymion," either in April or May, 1817, at Carisbrooke. He continued it at Margate and Oxford—once at the rate of a thousand lines in three weeks—and finished it in November at Burford Bridge. By the time he had revised it and came to write a preface for it in April 1818, he saw it as showing "great inexperience, immaturity, and every error denoting a feverish attempt, rather than a deed accomplished," but beyond revision; for "the foundations are too sandy." Fancies of the poet-lover who "gave meek Cynthia her Endymion" had formed part of "I stood tip-toe." "Endymion" was, in fact, built on the same foundations as the "Poems" of 1817. To make a long narrative poem seemed to him, a great lover of "The Faerie Queene," "Paradise Lost," and "The Excursion," to be a right and high thing. It became also a sort of allegory of the spiritual development which he forecast for himself. Narrative and allegory alike are buried deep in the beautiful flowers scattered over them profusely and confusedly. The whole is not a meal, but a week's rations, of claret and ratafia cakes, apart from certain too loosely connected passages of difficult thinking, for which prayer and fasting are the only preparation. No poem of the same length is so crammed with loveliness and love of loveliness. No English poem is so impossible to read through with a sense of anything in it before and after the lines immediately under the eye. The parts, so far from aiding one another, are rivals. Moreover, each part is broken up by the multitude of details which in any case would have been difficult of connection, and also by a lack of continuity in construction, no doubt fostered by the habit of dealing with separate beauties instead of organic ideas ; while a trick of style, which puts a full stop anywhere but at the end of a line, only exaggerates this discontinuity. Add to these objections, that as thick as the beauties are the expressions of incontinent, soft feeling, the languors and luxuries, which might almost have been spread over the beauties, in the absence of one sustained imaginative impulse and emotion, to give them life.

Imagine the masque in "The Tempest," imagine the opening words of Iris and Ceres, multiplied fifty times : the four thousand lines, even from Shakespeare's hand, could hardly have been much more sumptuous and fresh at once than "Endymion," though they would have been less luscious. Wherever Keats has an opportunity, as in the chorus of Pan's worshippers, of knitting his choice things together, he does so, with a country basket like this :

> "O thou to whom
> Broad-leaved fig-trees even now foredoom
> Their ripen'd fruitage; yellow girted bees
> Their golden honeycombs; our village leas
> Their fairest blossom'd beans and poppied corn;
> The chuckling linnet its five young unborn,
> To sing for thee; low creeping strawberries
> Their summer coolness; pent up butterflies
> Their freckled wings;"

still more in this loftier strain:

> "O Hearkener to the loud-clapping shears,
> While ever and anon to his shorn peers
> A ram goes bleating: Winder of the horn,
> When snouted wild-boars routing tender corn
> Anger our huntsmen; Breather round our farms,
> To keep off mildews and all weather harms:
> Strange ministrant of undescribed sounds
> That come a swooning over hollow grounds,
> And wither drearily on barren moors:
> Dread opener of the mysterious doors
> Leading to universal knowledge—see,
> Great son of Dryope,
> The many that are come to pay their vows
> With leaves about their brows!"

This is the thoroughly and rustically English, "Greek" style of the Elizabethans, and but for those "undescribed sounds" and "mysterious doors" might have come from the same hand as

> "You nymphs, called Naiads, of the wandering brooks,
> With your sedged crowns and ever harmless looks . . ."

But he had a sense of other things, such as brought

"round the heart an indescribable feud" and "dizzy pain," on beholding the Elgin Marbles. In Lemprière's classical dictionary he would have read how Orion rid Chios of wild beasts in order to gain the king's daughter, Hero, and how the king made him drunk and put out his eyes as he lay asleep on the seashore, and how Orion, putting a man on his back to guide him, went to where he could turn his eyes towards the east, and how the rising sun gave him back his sight. Keats, merely for a comparison, made the lines,

> "Like old Deucalion mountain'd o'er the flood,
> Or blind Orion hungry for the morn."

It is not the Shakesperian sublime, nor quite the Miltonic, but sublime it is. In the first of these two styles some of the most satisfying things in "Endymion" are written, and particularly the Indian maiden's description of Bacchus and his crew, merry beyond the dreams of Titian, high fantastical too, and magical when the Satyrs answer the questioners:

> "For wine, for wine we left our kernel tree;
> For wine we left our heath and yellow brooms,
> And cold mushrooms . . ."

There is also a third style, the style of Cupid's invitation to Endymion, where Shakespeare and Milton blend with Keats:

> "Here is wine
> Alive with sparkles—never, I aver,
> Since Ariadne was a vintager,

So cool a purple : taste these juicy pears,
Sent me by sad Vertumnus, when his fears
Were high about Pomona : here is cream,
Deepening to richness from a snowy gleam ;
Sweeter than that nurse Amalthes skimm'd
For the boy Jupiter: and here, undimm'd
By any touch, a bunch of blooming plums
Ready to melt between an infant's gums :
And here is manna pick'd from Syrian trees,
In starlight, by the three Hesperides."

There is a fourth, an almost French, witty, and decorated style, foreshadowing that of "Lamia," as in the speech of Venus :

"Visit thou my Cythera : thou wilt find
Cupid well-natured, my Adonis kind,"

and the picture of

"Courteous fountains to all cups outreach'd ;
And plunder'd vines, teeming exhaustless, pleach'd
New growth about each shell and pendent lyre ; "

which is like the ceiling of the Opera house in Paris, and at the opposite extreme from the magic which Keats exhibited for the first time in "Endymion."

The prevailing beauty is twofold. It is composed first of natural things of every order between the vast and the small, the vast often attaining the grandeur of that

"One fair palace, that far, far surpass'd,
Even for common bulk, those olden three,
Memphis, and Babylon and Nineveh : "

the small, often to the magic sweetness of

> "Honey from out the gnarled hive I'll bring
> And apples wan with sweetness, gather thee,—
> Cresses that grow where no man may them see,
> And sorrel untorn by the dew-clawed stag."

The second element is the human, usually blent with the other, but distinguished by utterances of philosophic solemnity that are really Keats's own, and by pictorial, statuesque, slender, and faintly unreal figures, who mingle divinity now with tragedy, now with arch comedy. Where this beauty has sway the verse disencumbers itself, running fresh as well as full, either massive or light and clear, with pauses of natural fitness whether at the end of a line or not, and possessing that frequent combination and interchange of vowels, as in

> "Let me have music dying, and I seek
> No more delight—I bid adieu to all,"

which had its source in his luxuriousness, aided no doubt, but never overmastered, by theory.

It is hardly necessary to dwell on the faults. The story has to be dug for with a determination which the conduct of it does not foster. In what obscures it lies the charm of the poem. That charm is itself modified by the lack of a harmonising unity and continuity, not merely in the narrative, but in the spirit. Still more is it modified by the frequent pauses to show us, as it turns out, not a picture, but a painter at work, as in this of Adonis:

"Not hiding up an Apollonian curve
Of neck and shoulder, nor the tenting swerve
Of knee from knee, or ankles pointing light ;
But rather, giving them to the filled sight
Officiously. Sideway his face repos'd
On one white arm, and tenderly unclos'd,
By tenderest pressure, a faint damask mouth
To slumbery pout : just as the morning south
Disparts a dew-lipp'd rose. . . ."

Worst fault of all is the incontinent collapse of luxury wherever a male and a female, or " white deliciousness," are brought together, as if, like Endymion, the poet himself

"had swoon'd
Drunken from pleasure's nipple."

It proves Keats right in his belief that he had not a right feeling about women : it suggests also that the wrong feeling was produced as much by the women with whom he was most familiar as by weakness innate in himself.

Natural beauty burns cold and sweet through this delicate grossness, but the abstract passages so important to Keats and to the purpose of the poem, are obscured and discredited by it. As it stands, these passages seem extracts from another poem, surprisingly like Wordsworth or Shelley in its overt intention, and altogether unlike a " pretty piece of Paganism." According to taste, they constitute the hugest mistake, or the chief virtue. Could they

"ENDYMION"

have been woven into the narrative and description, so that the philosophy and the poem were one, "Endymion" must have been one of the great beautiful poems of the world, instead of one of the fullest of beauties.

CHAPTER IV

"ISABELLA," "LAMIA," "THE EVE OF ST. AGNES," AND THE ODES

IMMEDIATELY on finishing "Endymion," Keats wrote "Isabella." He was then disturbed by the sailing of his brother and sister-in-law to America. The walking tour followed, and he wrote a few sonnets, some pedestrian verses, and "Meg Merrilies." When he had been a month back in Hampstead "Endymion" was attacked by the *Quarterly Review*. A month later he met Fanny Brawne. Then his brother Tom died. So passed the year 1818. That winter he began "Hyperion" and within a year it had been abandoned and most of the poems written which were published with it in July 1820, together with "La Belle Dame sans Merci" and more of the finest work which remained unpublished at his death.

"Isabella," so soon after "Endymion," was already a masterpiece. It was the first long poem in which Keats put all his luxury, all his pitifulness, in perfect order and combination, and the more effective for being subordinated to the clear telling of a story which was in itself sufficiently interesting. It has

"ISABELLA," "LAMIA," ETC.

some excess of explicit pallor and tenderness, but, for the rest, the poet's pity blends with the happiness, then the sorrow, of his characters, with the richness and splendour of things mentioned—the broidery, the hyacinth and musk, June, the "warm Indian clove," "roses amorous of the moon," the "middays of Autumn," the "spangly gloom," "the ancient harps," "Araby," "sad Melpomene," and the like—and with the still greater richness and splendour in the sound of the verses. The stanza form helped in two ways. It was a discipline that forbade loose running on: it exhibited the poet's choiceness of detail better than the couplets of "Endymion," and, at the same time, each stanza being complete in itself gave more excuse for it. There had been no such layer upon layer of richness, corporeal and incorporeal, since Spenser. It was reserved for Keats to make tragedy a luxury that had its own fit company of luxurious things appealing to sight, hearing, touch, and scent, in art and nature; and although a story was involved, "Isabella" became, with the help of the *adagio* stanza, a very still poem, as if all that takes place in its "quiet glooms" were seen as Isabella saw Lorenzo's spirit:

"As when of healthful midnight sleep bereft,
    Thinking on rugged hours and fruitless toil,
We put our eyes into a pillowy cleft,
    And see the spangly gloom froth up and boil . . ."

as if the poet was somehow sequestered, like the dead Lorenzo who saw his mistress "distant in Humanity."

The inactive pity, the unreluctant and even complacent melancholy, that see in the increasing sorrow of their heroine or victim a richer zest, were new then to poetry, though the nineteenth century staled them. For the moment of this passage:

> "Great bliss was with them, and great happiness
> Grew, like a lusty flower in June's caress.
>
> Parting they seem'd to tread upon the air,
>   Twin roses by the zephyr blown apart,
> Only to meet again more close, and share
>   The inward fragrance of each other's heart.
> She, to her chamber gone, a ditty fair
>   Sang, of delicious love and honey'd dart;
> He with light steps went up a western hill,
> And bade the sun farewell, and joy'd his fill";

for one moment the sun strikes across the mouth of this dim, melodious cave, making its dimness thicker and more opulent. For, says the poet, "there is richest juice in poison-flowers." Thus all Keats's vivacity and judgment, and clear, determined thinking about man and nature, seem to have weighed less than that sense of the miseries of the world which came upon him when he reflected that he was to die, and that " women have cancers."

Keats seldom, after " Isabella," wrote a poem where this sense does not prevail, however quietly. Even " To Fancy " is a kind of incantation or receipt against it:

> "Let the wingèd Fancy roam;
>   Pleasure never is at home."

"ISABELLA," "LAMIA," ETC.

It was in the measure of the two earlier poems on the Mermaid Tavern and Robin Hood. Written while " Endymion " was being finished, these were among the last done in the social spirit of the epistles and other poems of 1817, yet they were cheerful mainly in retrospect, upon a groundwork of regret :

"Silent is the ivory shrill
Past the heath and up the hill.
There is no mid-forest laugh
Where lone Echo gives the half
To some wight, amazed to hear
Jesting, deep in forest drear."

There is yet another, contained in a letter to Reynolds, of February 1818 ; it is a translation of a thrush's song that told him he was " right to have no idea but of the morning " :

" O fret not after knowledge ! I have none,
And yet my song comes native with the warmth.
O fret not after knowledge ! I have none,
And yet the evening listens. He who saddens
At thought of idleness cannot be idle,
And he's awake who thinks himself asleep."

The great odes, the poem to Autumn, and " The Eve of St. Agnes," could never have been translated out of a thrush's song. Love for vanished, inaccessible, inhuman things, almost for death itself—regret —and the consolations offered by the intensity which makes pleasure and pain so much alike—are the principal moods of these poems. Such action as there is in " The Eve of St. Agnes " is far more subdued than that in " Isabella " : it is no more than is necessary to bring a man and woman together alone, luxuriously, in perfect love, in a soft chamber, islanded in the midst of noisy, ribald enemies and a wild winter night—" of haggard seeming, but a boon indeed " to poet and lovers. It ends :

> " And they are gone: aye, ages long ago
> These lovers fled away into the storm."

More richly and more completely than in " Isabella " are all possible choice, lovely, and sweet things here mingled, expressed in words with sounds and associations equalling them for choiceness, loveliness, sweetness.

The " Eve of St. Agnes " is the most perfect thing of its kind written by Keats or any other poet. Though long, it is not too long : it can be browsed on, but not skipped. In fact it is impossible to suppose that poetry of this immobile, sumptuous, antiquarian kind can go beyond it. Among Keats's poems it equals the best odes and " La Belle Dame sans Merci," but is likely at times to be placed above them.

The " Ode to Psyche " has an element of narrative and dialogue. It was " the first and the only one," said Keats as he copied it for his brother in April 1819, with which he had taken " even moderato pains " : " St. Agnes' Eve " was then awaiting the revision given to it, as we know, with more than moderate pains. He was, he said, " more orthodox than to let a heathen Goddess be so neglected " as Psyche had been in classical times. The narrative

"ISABELLA," "LAMIA," ETC. 53

passages are like the best in "Endymion." The poem rises from "delicious moan" to where

> "dark-clustered trees
> Fledge the wild-ridged mountains steep by steep,"

only to place there a sanctuary, with

> "A bright torch, and a casement ope at night,
> To let the warm Love in";

and so ends—having touched every mood of "Endymion" swiftly and exquisitely—with a dramatic archness. "To Autumn," also, it would be perverse to class with "Isabella" mainly on account of the customary sadness of Autumn, the use of "soft-dying," "wailful," "mourn," and "dies," in the last verse, and in the last line,

> "And gathering swallows twitter in the skies"—

something light, thin, cold, and vanishing, especially by comparison with the mellowness and slowness of the other verses, with all their long "oo" and "ou" and "aw" and "z" sounds, as in the line,

> "Thou watchest the last oozings hours by hours."

The "Ode on Melancholy" is one of the central poems of this period, admitting, as it does so fully, and celebrating, the relationship between melancholy and certain still pleasures. Nowhere is the connoisseurship of the quiet, withdrawn spectator so extremely and remorselessly put. The "rich anger" of the mistress is to be a precious, delicious object; her "peerless eyes" are to be devoured as roses.

Richer juice could not be extracted from poison-flowers. Miss Mary Suddard, one of his best critics, says that "Keats, like Jaques, spent his whole life chewing the cud of sweet and bitter fancy, and, still more, of sweet and bitter sensation"; and the poem, taken literally, seems to say that the bitter with the sweet is worth while—is the necessary woof of life—and makes for the fulness of the banquet, which is so gorgeous that death seems its solemn closing music, and it is "rich to die." In short, he flatters life and the bitterness of it, and men that have to drink it. Since the Greeks called the Furies the Blessed Ones there has been no choicer flattery of life. Like the other odes, but above them, this one on Melancholy touches the summit of expression for what Miss Suddard called the "ruminant" nature.

"To a Nightingale" is in the same tone, except that it has an outdoor setting, and is tinged with action, and comes to an end with a slow restoration of every-day light and with a question. Nor does it pretend to content. There is a pain in the numbness, a desire of escape from the "embalmed darkness," an impatience of any end to the banquet saving death. Yet the variety in the richness of the poem is made by that very pain, desire, and impatience. To complain of the opening,

"My heart aches, and a drowsy numbness pains
My sense, as though of hemlock I had drunk,"

is useless. For England does not send poets into exile with crowns; our civilisation is by no means assured what is good and what is evil, and whether the evil is to be rejected, since, after all, men are lower than the angels. Only a very bold man, outside a pulpit, would pronounce that such poetry infects life and literature. What is most excellent in its kind establishes that kind. You cannot prove that this poem hastens the decay of those who incline towards such things in life and in literature; still less, that to take it away is to arrest their falling. Many that admire it have no such inclination, and will suffer from a vision of these things at best no more than men in the old days suffered by thinking of Paradise. Instead of corrupting them it will deepen their taste of life, and perhaps also their understanding. They will enjoy it; their enjoyment of very different things, like Pindar's or Shelley's poetry, will be increased. But I am not attempting to answer the man who should say that after boiling the "Ode to a Nightingale," he found only peevishness at the bottom of it. I do think, however, that melancholy (in spite of the ode) is too disparaging a name for this mood, and that we have been deceived into suspecting evil of the poem because it is beautiful and attributes divinity to what we think a weakness. None to-day would complain if the thought had remained in this lyrical form:

> "Welcome joy, and welcome sorrow,
>   Lethe's weed and Hermes' feather!
> Come to-day, and come to-morrow;
>   I do love you both together";

we should begin to talk earnestly of the gospel of pain.

I shall not set about a demonstration from the beginning that the ode truly is one of the things that are most excellent. I will, however, mention one indication of its excellence. It and the "Ode on a Grecian Urn" are of a texture so consummate and consistent that the simple line,

"The grass, the thicket, and the fruit-tree wild,"

in one of them, and an equally simple line in the other,

"With forest branches, and the trodden weed,"

both gain from their environment an astonishing beauty, profound and touching.

The "Ode on a Grecian Urn" is preferred, by some people and some moods, to the "Nightingale" and the rest, because it is the most universal and intellectual, the calmest as well as the stillest, of all. Its personality is submerged, and the more intense for that. The poet flatters the figures on the urn because they are dead and fixed in attitudes of desire, so that they will never suffer like living men,

"a heart high-sorrowful and cloy'd,
A burning forehead, and a parching tongue,"

and forasmuch as they have the intensity of beauty which can "tease us out of thought" into their own marble blessedness. The poem has two doubtful blemishes, the suggestion of a pun in "O Attic shape! Fair attitude!" and the odd break in the last line but one which compels us to attribute

"Beauty is Truth, Truth Beauty,"

to the Urn, and

"—that is all
Ye know on earth, and all ye need to know,"

to the poet. But this last may be an accidental typographical error, and these things rarely, as a matter of fact, modify in the least degree the impression left. The poem also is free from all but the lightest touch of the morbidity of "Melancholy" and the "Nightingale," if indeed "a burning forehead and a parching tongue" and "for ever panting" are felt as morbid—I incline to think they are universal as the rest, as the whole is.

Thus in the odes the poet made for himself a form in which the essence of all his thought, feeling, and observation, could be stored without overflowing or disorder; of its sources in his daily life there was no more shown than made his poems quick instead of dead. Their perfection is like that of a few of Milton's and Spenser's poems. They are among the unquestionable mortal achievements. "On Indolence" would have been another, could it have had Keats's final revision: as it is, the line,

"A pet lamb in a sentimental farce,"

and not that alone, confronts us with the writer's daily life, restoring the atmosphere of the letter where he speaks of that "delightful sensation, about three degrees on this side of faintness," in which apparently the ode was conceived.

"Lamia," written in July and September 1819, is a narrative poem almost as different as possible from "Isabella." The story, clear, well-balanced, and essential, gives form to the substantial beauty of the whole. The masculine side of Keats, supported by a study of John Dryden, has the upper hand in it. The nymph, indeed, is timorous and faint to excess at the approach of Hermes, but the poet's comment,

> " Into the green-recessed woods they flew ;
> Nor grew they pale, as mortal lovers do,"

has an adult cynic humour, and but for

> " There is not such a treat among them all—
> Haunters of cavern, lake, and waterfall—
> As a real woman . . ."

his attitude is firm as well as masculine throughout. He was in the mood of his sonnet on Fame, where he bids poets " repay her scorn for scorn "—a little below the masculine loftiness of the sonnet. Even where Keats is obviously speaking it is in a more intellectual and assured tone, almost as much unlike himself as Dryden was unlike Shakespeare :

> " There was an awful rainbow once in heaven ;
> We know her woof, her texture ; she is given
> In the dull catalogue of common things.
> Philosophy will clip an angel's wings . . ."

Everything is hard and clear, many things splendid. It would have satisfied the age of Dryden almost as well as it does our own. And that is not quite perfectly. To some extent the poem was a *tour de force* in an external, "classical" style. There were approaches to it in "Endymion," while "Cap and Bells" is a further development, where the decadence is plain. I think "Lamia" contains the symptoms of the decadence. It tastes somewhat of metal, not, like "La Belle Dame sans Merci," written a little before it, of "honey wild." The ballad form, also, of "La Belle Dame" was slightly foreign to Keats: it helped his lighter, freer, less congested style— the style of "Robin Hood" and of "O sorrow, sorrow," the one purely lyric song in "Endymion" —to meet the style of the odes, to a result only equalled among the odes. More than in them his thought and experience were subdued; they were suppressed; yet they were not destroyed, for it is one of the wisest poems of the world. Beauty, transiency, and dissatisfied desire, speak through it, and that in a narrative which is quintessential, yet as light as a lyric. It is the lightest of all Keats's poems.

Almost equally different from "Lamia," yet of that period, is the fragment of "The Eve of St. Mark." The contrasted richness is like that of "St. Agnes' Eve," which was being written during the same months of 1819, but with a tone and metre domestic rather than stately, by comparison. But so far as the poet went, he seems to have become entangled in visible things not sufficiently under control to be effective, except separately and one by one. It anticipates the pre-Raphaelites, but with a fresh early savour. It might have grown to a poem as much like "Christabel" as another poem could be. Some of the false impressiveness of a torso that never was a whole clings about it. But the "unmatur'd green valleys cold, the azure saints and silver rays," and the solitary maiden, Bertha,

"with bright drooping hair
And slant book, full against the glare.
Her shadow, in uneasy guise,
Hovered about, a giant size,
On ceiling beam and old oak chair,
The parrot's cage, and panel square;
And the warm angled winter-screen,
On which were many monsters seen,
Call'd doves of Siam, Lima mice, . . ."

these were, in spite of Chatterton, practically new things, and better than all of the same kind that came after them. Finally, Keats must have the credit of abandoning the poem. Why he did so is unknown. Perhaps "Cap and Bells," where several Berthas and St. Mark's Eve are mentioned, crossed the path of the poem and scared it and its "spirit of town quietude." Or it may be simply that he felt it tapering off too slenderly to give more than "the sensation of walking about an old country town in a coolish evening"; so he spoke of it in September 1819 at Winchester.

CHAPTER V

"HYPERION" AND THE LAST SONNET

IT was at this time that Keats was planning to live at Westminster and turn journalist. He had finished "Lamia." and "St. Agnes' Eve" and that social task, "Otho the Great," performed with the stage directly in view, but destined to disappointment. The great fertile concentration of a year was breaking up. Fanny Brawne was gaining upon him. In that same September "Hyperion" was put aside. With the fragment of it, the volume of 1820 ended.

Keats himself said that he put it aside because of the Miltonisms of style in it. Possibly the spirit that finished "Lamia" was incompatible with "Hyperion." The poet was towering in "Hyperion." The divine theme had lured him, like "Endymion," into what he might have felt too open and direct a declaration of his own thought, as when Oceanus says:

"We fall by course of Nature's law, not force
 Of thunder, or of Jove . . ."

and

"'Tis the eternal law
That first in beauty should be first in might."

He had not dimmed the brightness of the gods, but the pale cast of thought had touched them. One of his powers is used, and perfectly, to paint the Titans in their " covert drear " :

> " Scarce images of life, one here, one there,
> Lay vast and edgeways; like a dismal cirque
> Of Druid stones, upon a forlorn moor,
> When the chill rain begins at shut of eve."

But this still life could not be stirred into speech and action without a dangerous transition of styles. These giant figures in repose, like " Druid stones," with " Druid locks," seem not meant for the same poem as when they are debating. The result of these differences and of the long human-thoughtful speeches is that the action is not greatly more epic than in " Endymion." Sometimes the speeches are of epic majesty, worthy of a poem that might have been second only to " Paradise Lost." Sometimes they are of a human softness and regretfulness, as in Saturn's

> " But I am smother'd up,
> And buried from all godlike exercise
> Of influence benign on planets pale,
> Of admonitions to the winds and seas,
> Of peaceful sway above man's harvesting,
> And all those acts which Deity supreme
> Doth ease its heart of love in,"

which goes better with the " Druid " atmosphere and suggests a Celtic narrative. This double character pervades the whole. There are godlike figures,

"HYPERION" AND LAST SONNET 63

attitudes, and utterances, but the poet's language and philosophy and grasp of life do not build up around them a world of suitable scale or atmosphere that is harmonious. Milton's immortals are Miltonic; they move in a Miltonic world. Keats's immortals are something not quite Keatsian, if less than Miltonic; they move in a Keatsian world. Not Miltonism of style, but an attempt at the Miltonic scale provoked by the style or suggested to the reader by it—that was Keats's danger. "Hyperion," abounding in great things, lacks consistent greatness. It seldom quite matches even where it equals the opening lines,

"Deep in the shady sadness of a vale
Far sunken from the healthy breath of morn,
Far from the fiery noon, and eve's one star,
Sat grey-hair'd Saturn, quiet as a stone,
Still as the silence round about his lair;
Forest on forest hung about his head
Like cloud on cloud. No stir of air was there,
Not so much life as on a summer's day
Robs not one light seed from the feather'd grass,
But where the dead leaf fell, there did it rest.
A stream went voiceless by, still deadened more
By reason of his fallen divinity
Spreading a shade: the Naiad 'mid her reeds
Press'd her cold finger closer to her lips,"

which are pure Keats, though even farther than the odes from the sumptuousness of "St. Agnes," perfect were it not for the rhymes, and "shady," "healthy," "fiery," in successive lines. Justly did

Keats say to his Muse at the beginning of the third book:

> "A solitary sorrow best befits
> Thy lips, and antheming a lonely grief."

Yet it is so near greatness that again and again it seems to have been achieved. It cannot but have meant an overpowering effort of ambition and imagination alike, to strive out of the world in which Keats could dwell so easily—the world of the picture of Saturn and Thea:

> "One moon, with alteration slow, had shed
> Her silver seasons four upon the night,
> And still these two were postured motionless,
> Like natural sculpture in cathedral cavern . . ."

into the world of angered Enceladus:

> "Or shall we listen to the over-wise,
> Or to the over-foolish giant, Gods? . . ."

from the scene of Apollo's wandering forth in Delos

> "Beside the osiers of a rivulet,
> Full ankle-deep in lilies of the vale.
> The nightingale had ceased, and a few stars
> Were lingering in the heavens, while the thrush
> Began calm-throated . . ."

to that palace bright,

> "Bastion'd with pyramids of glowing gold,
> And touch'd with shade of bronzed obelisks . . ."

It was one thing to weep, in a sonnet,

> "That I have not the cloudy winds to keep
> Fresh for the opening of the morning's eye";

another to paint the sun-giant sorrowing as

> "all along a dismal rack of clouds,
> Upon the boundaries of day and night,
> He stretch'd himself in grief and radiance faint."

The effort brought forth things mighty enough to have commanded Byron's respect, whether he meant what he said in "Don Juan" or not. But for "shady sadness," the opening scene, and the divine figures, and the first speeches, to where Thea leads away Saturn, are most noble and in a manner entirely Keats's own. The scale, in spite of the statement,

> "Her face was large as that of Memphian sphinx,"

is human. Saturn is a venerable, antique king, of Lear's stature. The landscape is of the earth, with that blending of the "Celtic" and "Greek," as Arnold called them, which is Keats; and the consummate style makes of these thirteen words,

> "The Naiad 'mid her reeds
> Press'd her cold finger closer to her lips,"

something more visible and alive than all "The Eve of St. Agnes" and "The Eve of St. Mark." Perhaps the first point of discord is where Saturn speaks of "influence benign on planets pale" and "the gold clouds metropolitan." Can it be the voice of that grey-haired Druid king? Another pause is at Hyperion's palace door,

> "like a rose in vermeil tint and shape,
> In fragrance soft, and coolness to the eye,"

which is too easily visualised, a cool, soft, fragrant, rose-like entrance of gigantic size, and as easily rejected. Then, gradually the lack of sustained continuity, the failure of the style, congested, much divided up, abrupt in its transitions, to give a sense of progress, leaves the reader in danger of being entangled in the many felicitous things, grand and beautiful, until he is disturbed by a piece of the supernatural, like

> "Above a sombre cliff
> Their heads appear'd, and up their stature grew,
> Till on the level height their steps found ease."

Wherever there is no action, but only an inanimate scene, or the effects of action or preparations for it, to be described, Keats is master; and, as more than once or twice in "Otho," so many times in "Hyperion," his style brings a great and a new music into the brain. His separate Titans and his groups,

> "Cœus, and Gyges, and Briareüs,
> Typhon, and Dolor, and Porphyrion,
> With many more, the brawniest in assault,"

prove it. It is proved by similes like

> "There is a roaring in the bleak-grown pines
> When Winter lifts his voice; there is a noise
> Among immortals when a God gives sign,
> With hushing finger, how he means to load
> His tongue with the full weight of utterless thought,
> With thunder, and with music, and with pomp:
> Such noise is like the roar of bleak-grown pines;
> Which, when it ceases in this mountain'd world,
> No other sound succeeds . . ."

That Keats knew his danger is shown by his ending a detailed picture of the Titans with

> "And many else whose names may not be told.
> For when the Muse's wings are air-ward spread,
> Who shall delay her flight ? "

The succeeding philosophic speeches of Saturn and Oceanus, with Clymene's pretty tale, are but the gentlest of flights. The sudden " Speak ! roar ! shout ! yell ! " of Enceladus reverberates over the silence of the poem like a bull roaring in a great combe. It wakes no action, except what is involved in the sublime picture of Hyperion arriving—with too Keats-like sighing—and all despondent until

> "Fierce Enceladus sent forth his eyes
> Among the brotherhood ; and at their glare,
> Uprose Iäpetus, and Creüs too,
> And Phorcus, sea-born, and together strode
> To where he towered on his eminence.
> There those four shouted forth old Saturn's name ;
> Hyperion from the peak loud answered, 'Saturn !'
> Saturn sat near the Mother of the Gods
> In whose face was no joy, though all the Gods
> Gave from their hollow throats the name of 'Saturn !'"

And is there not, in this ever so faintly humorous stir, something boyish, perhaps in keeping with the Titans' natures, but less so with the spirit which the poem has at this point created ?

It is impossible to say whether Keats could have lifted the inert mass much farther. He was describing action when the poem was put aside, but describing it with an intruded " lo ! " as if to increase its vividness by the suggestion that he was himself a witness:

> "At length
> Apollo shriek'd—and lo! from all his limbs
> Celestial Glory dawn'd: he was a god!"

So he had written. Perhaps the feebleness of " he was a god " was the last straw of his dissatisfaction, and the words after " celestial " were cut out. In " Hyperion " Keats failed greatly, instead of succeeding moderately as in the drama of " Otho the Great."

Before the end of 1819 Keats set about re-writing " Hyperion," and from what he did it is clear that something more than its Miltonism had displeased him in the first draft. The new version was in the form of a dream. It was to contain, apparently, much the same events, speeches, and scenery, as the old. In this way, the lack of concrete active qualities of style, and the corresponding dearth of action and progress, might have ceased to disable the poem. Not enough was done to fortify the new form. It suffers from a general thinning of style. It is infirm with thoughts, at times openly didactic, like Wordsworth; at others, touched too closely with general and personal sadness: so that really there is something more than sick modesty in the lines:

> "Whether the dream now purposed to rehearse
> Be poet's or fanatic's will be known
> When this warm scribe, my hand, is in the grave."

"HYPERION" AND LAST SONNET

For Keats, now back at Hampstead, ill, and near the beginning of his fatal illness, was, for the moment at least, fanatically one of those who alone, in the Dream, might ascend to Moneta's shrine,

> "Those to whom the miseries of the world
> Are misery, and will not let them rest."

The man who declared fine writing, next to fine doing, "the top thing in the world," knelt to a lecturess, saying :

> "What benefit canst thou do, or all thy tribe,
> To the great world ? Thou art a dreaming thing,
> A fever of thyself ! Think of the earth ;
> What bliss, even in hope, is there for thee ?
> What haven ? every creature hath its home,
> Every sole man hath days of joy and pain,
> Whether his labours be sublime or low—
> The pain alone, the joy alone, distinct :
> Only the dreamer venoms all his days,
> Bearing more woe than all his sins deserve."

His pitifulness was grown incontinent. Saturn now appeared to him, not a Druid, or a Lear, at least; but complains like

> "some poor old man of the earth
> Bewailing earthly loss."

More than once appears a strange timorousness. Moneta inspires the dreamer with "a terror of her robes"; the pallor of her cheeks when she unveils them passed "the lily and the snow," but he says :

"beyond these
I must not think now, though I saw that face."

Then, as Saturn and Thea depart, and Moneta goes on to speak, the dreamer adds:

> "As ye may read who can unwearied pass
> Onward from the antechamber of this dream,
> Where, even at the open doors, awhile
> I must delay, and glean my memory
> Of her high phrase—perhaps no further dare."

Whether a real dread, or a pretended or exaggerated one, was the occasion of the last four words, they seem to spring from some serious weakness.

Keats's decline is more painful in the jaunty mock-heroics of "Cap and Bells" than in the sadness of the revised "Hyperion." "Cap and Bells" was being written at the same time. Onward through that last spring at Brown's house he was thinking with pleasure of the fun of the thing, but intending to revise it and to leave nothing to reproach himself with. It is a vile failure. Keats, with all his intellectual humour and his sound sense, could not, when it came to poetry, do anything like "The Witch of Atlas" or "Peter Bell the Third." He exposed the same weakness of taste as, on the serious side, he did in "Endymion"; he became jaunty and worse, but meant to sign himself "Lucy Vaughan Lloyd."

Thereafter Keats wrote frantic personal pieces incapable of being finished, with Fanny Brawne before him, Death behind him. This was executioner Death or doctor Death, the "great divorcer," not Death the "luxury" which was "Life's high meed," as he used to think in his days of nature. But one great poem was stored up for him to write, in this posture between Death and his mistress, in September of that year :

> "Bright star, would I were steadfast as thou art,
>   Not in lone splendour hung aloft the night
> And watching, with eternal lids apart,
>   Like nature's patient, sleepless Eremite,
> The moving waters at their priestlike task
>   Of pure ablution round earth's human shores,
> Or gazing on the new soft-fallen mask
>   Of snow upon the mountains and the moors—
> No—yet still steadfast, still unchangeable,
>   Pillow'd upon my fair love's ripening breast,
> To feel for ever its soft fall and swell,
>   Awake for ever in a sweet unrest,
> Still, still to hear her tender-taken breath,
> And so live ever—or else swoon to death."

The sublimity of the opening lends itself to the conclusion. The earth becomes his pillow, the air his winding-sheet, the sea "a mighty minstrel" that can hush "the tempest cares of life," and death, yet once more "easeful" death, a twin luxury to his mistress's beauty. For in his heyday of poetry, thirteen months before at Winchester, he had told his mistress that he had two luxuries to brood over in his walks, her loveliness and the hour of his death, and exclaimed, "Oh, that I could have possession of them both in the same minute!" And now, at the beginning of his "posthumous life," thinking the same, the sonnet was written. It is the hymn of stillness, equalising the steadfast watching star, and the poet that saw likewise, and the lover with assuaged passion, less than "three parts this side of faintness," and the dead body which some also envy for the tranquillity of the skin. The snow spreads like winter's grave-cloth over the earth. The star hangs vigilant and regardless. Keats was not talking when he told Fanny Brawne that Love was his religion. This is the hymn of stillness, of voluptuous rest, mystically praising love and death together. It is one of Keats's greatest poems, but distinguished from the others—"St. Agnes," the Odes, and "La Belle Dame"—by the break in the rhythm and the voice in the last line, as if life intruded—or, rather, death. This end of his poetry was fitting. Perfect language, endowed with a more sweeping rhythmic energy than was usual in his work, builds up a vision of sky and earth, immense in its grandeur and its calm ; and in the midst of it a man troubled by the principal unrest of life cries out for that same calm, for the oblivion of "melting out his essence fine into the winds," for "soothest sleep that saves from curious conscience," for the happiness of the seeming immortal nightingale, of the "marble men and maidens" carved on the urn, the dead poets "on Elysian lawns" who know not satiety, for the intensity of great art. Oppressed by disease and misfortune, the poet seems to choose death rather than life. "To make beauty," says Dr. A. C. Bradley, "was his philanthropy." The poem, for living men, adds a beauty to life and a new ground for desiring it.

CHAPTER VI

CHARACTER

THESE last months of dissolution coupled with the most obvious qualities of his earlier poems have given colour to a belief that Keats was an invertebrate, one to be "snuffed out by an article." He was himself the first discoverer of that "morbidity of temperament." That he did discover it, that he had a wonderful self-knowledge—not mere self-analysis—calm and penetrating, never coldly submissive, is a proof that it was not the whole truth. The morbidity was the occasional overbalancing of his intense sympathy, his greatest passive power. He thought that men of genius in general had no individuality; they were "everything and nothing"; they were theatres where others' tragedies and comedies were enacted; they were distinguished by what he called Negative Capability—"that is, when a man is capable of being in uncertainties, mysteries, doubts, without any irritable reaching after fact and reason." "Let us," he said to Reynolds, "be passive and receptive, like a flower, budding patiently under the eye of Apollo, and taking hints from every noble mind that pays us a visit."

CHARACTER

He was for a " delicious diligent indolence," for a passiveness allowing the intellectual powers to come very gradually to ripeness. When he was in a room with people, unless he was following a definite thought, he was so open to their influence that the identity of everyone pressed on him and annihilated him : the identity of his sick brother pressed on him until he was obliged to go out or to " plunge into abstract images " to save himself; while the deep impression made on him by the identity of his brother George and his sister-in-law helped him to a " direct communication of spirit " with them across the Atlantic. When he was alone the shapes of poetry came to him, and, according to his state of mind, he was with Achilles or Theocritus; repeating the words of Troilus,

"I stalk about her door
Like a strange soul upon the Stygian banks
Staying for waftage,"

he melted into the air " with a voluptuousness so delicate " that he was content to be alone. Lifelike, but more lasting than life, was his imagining of " Alcibiades leaning on his Crimson Couch in his Galley, his broad shoulders imperceptibly heaving with the sea," or of the scene,

"See how the surly Warwick mans the Wall."

If these things were too persistent they became " day nightmares." So he could lie awake listening to the night rain " with a sense of being drowned and rotted like a grain of wheat"; if a sparrow came before his window he could "take part in its existence and pick about the gravel"; and he has said that the poet is one

> "who with a bird,
> Wren or eagle, finds his way to
> All its instincts . . ."

So also he entered into the serpent's brain with Satan and suffocated in the confinement. No wonder that the return of a friend, when he had had two days' luxuriating in solitude and silence, broke on him "like a thunderbolt," or that the images during the intensity of composition could keep Fanny Brawne at a distance, or that he could see his need for a sound heart and the lungs of an ox " to bear unhurt the shock of extreme thought and sensation without weariness," and, thus equipped, could contemplate living very nearly alone for a long life. At one time he left off animal food, as he said, that his " teeming brain" might not be in a greater mist than was natural to it. And there seems no doubt that this intense life of the mind often reached a point either of aching or of languor. The word "ache" is one of his constant, significant words. He ached to be near Fanny Brawne and to be with her; his arms ached to be round her waist; his senses ached at the haunting vision of her in a shepherdess dress, as they did at that passage in "Paradise Lost." In the ode "On Melancholy" Pleasure is "aching Pleasure"; "To a Nightingale" opens with "My heart aches"; he "ached for wings" in "On Indolence"; Hyperion ached with horrors; the Titans' exile was an "aching time" to Thea; Apollo, as yet realmless and imperfectly divine, was idle "in aching ignorance"; at thought of how the sculptured dead ached in his frosty chapel the old Beadsman's spirit failed, in "The Eve of St. Agnes"; the earth trodden on by his Auranthe is "the amorous-aching earth" to Ludolph; and Theodore "ached to think" of the horrors that were to come.

The recurrence of this word, "ache," suggests that the state which it describes was familiar to Keats, perhaps in the extremes of intense sensation and imagination—in such times as when the thousand images passing through his brain helped to spread the veil between him and Fanny Brawne, when he was "in complete cue—in the fever." Thus, to attain a poem, he went through something like the pains necessary to life, to what he thought the world's great task of making souls. Nothing that could foster intensity was alien to him. "King Lear," he knew, was the richer for its tears. The greater the truth, the greater the beauty, provided it was beauty—provided, that is to say, that it was handled with the intensity of imagination which makes "all disagreeables evaporate." Hence, "Beauty is Truth, Truth Beauty," and his saying that the excellence of every art is its intensity. Thought he respected, but not old clothes. He asked,

"What sea bird o'er the sea
Is a philosopher the while he goes
Winging along where the great water throes?"

and he wished poetry to be as unencumbered as that, having no palpable design upon the reader— as a tiger moth, clean and clear of the chrysalis. The " egotistical sublime " of Wordsworth and the philanthropy of Shelley were distasteful to him as an artist because, and in so far as, they endangered that rich, lucid, unprejudiced perfection which he himself desired. The poetry that reached this perfection wrung him to the point of believing that " fine writing is, next to fine doing, the top thing in the world."

That this man, with these thoughts, should—as Mr. Stopford Brooke believes he did—" forget the weary and the heavy weight of the unintelligible, and dwelling in the absolute beauty live and breathe in joy," is improbable. Sermons, political speeches, parlour conversations, and other things muddied by ignoble as well as noble desires, and lacking in truth and beauty, might weary him. But he loved life too well to turn his back on anything by which men were moved. His danger was to see and care for too many things, entertained as he was by " the alertness of the Stoat or the anxiety of a Deer," and capable of admitting both that a street quarrel was hateful, but the energies displayed in it fine, since " the commonest Man shows a grace in his quarrel." He shut his eyes neither to Charmian, nor to Bishop Hooker rocking his child's cradle, nor to " the Duchess of Dunghill " on the road from Belfast :

"A squalid old woman, squat like an ape half-starved, from a scarcity of biscuit in its passage from Madagascar to

CHARACTER

the Cape, with a pipe in her mouth, and looking out with a round-eyed, skinny-lidded inanity ; with a sort of horizontal idiotic movement of her head—squat and lean, she sat, and puffed out the smoke . . ."

For very long tracts of time Keats was one of the soberest, soundest, keenest, and most kindly brains that ever considered man and God. If he desired, on the one hand, "not to see beyond our bourne," and, on the other, "to do the world some good," he wasted no time on either as a deliberate task. His poetry shows his concern for Freedom, for the lot of those who toil

"In torched mines and noisy factories,"

for the death of

"The seal on the cold ice with piteous bark,"

for the

"people of no name,
In noisome alley, and in pathless wood,"

who are not incapable of highmindedness and singleness of aim above the "money-mongering and pitiable brood" : it shows also his dislike of church bells and the "sermon's horrid sound," for which men will quit the "converse high of those with glory crown'd" : above all, it shows his consciousness that he must pass on from "Flora and old Pan" to

"a nobler life,
Where he may find the agonies, the strife
Of human hearts ;"

and the one fairly clear and continuous interest in "Endymion" is the wandering of the hero out of a dream in which he loved a goddess, into a world of pains which he helps to relieve, and his union with a woman who is the goddess of his first dream disguised. The sound of the sea made him think of "what has been and will be," and, moreover, of those with "eyeballs vex'd and tired," or "ears dinn'd with uproar rude," whom the sea might comfort. At sight of Pan's dancing worshippers, youths and maidens, he exclaims :

"Fair creatures ! whose young children's children bred
   Thermopylæ its heroes . . ."

When Endymion praises love and its "ardent listlessness," he says it is because he has always thought

"that it might bless
The world with benefits unknowingly ;
As does the nightingale up-perched high
And cloister'd among cool and bunched leaves—
She sings but to her love, nor e'er conceives
How tiptoe Night holds back her dark-grey hood.
Just so may love, although 'tis understood
The mere commingling of passionate breath,
Produce more than our searching witnesseth."

This was no idle boy "with a child's amazement and forgetfulness."¹ For him it could have been no borrowed fancy that the award of posterity to the bard was richer than his living pleasures :

"What though I leave this dull and earthly mould,
   Yet shall my spirit lofty converse hold
   With after times.—The patriot shall feel
   My stern alarum, and unsheath his steel ;

Or in the senate thunder out my numbers,
To startle princes from their easy slumbers. . . .
Gay villagers, upon a morn of May,
When they have tired their gentle limbs with play
And form'd a snowy circle on the green,
And placed in midst of all that lovely lass
Who chosen is their queen,—with her fine head
Crowned with flowers purple, white and red:
For there the lily and the musk-rose sighing,
Are emblems true of hapless lovers dying:
Between her breasts, that never yet felt trouble,
A bunch of violets full blown, and double,
Serenely sleep : she from a casket takes
A little book,—and then a joy awakes
About each youthful heart,—with stifled cries,
And rubbing of white hands, and sparkling eyes :
For she's to read a tale of hopes and fears;
One that I foster'd in my youthful years. . . ."

Keats's letters make it doubly certain that these things were no more dreams, in any bad sense, than they were acts of Parliament. True, he liked to keep clear of parties, in literature and politics, and was sometimes contemptuous, like many wiser men who now yearn back to that day, of the " sickly safety and comfort " of his own time, and would say, under the joint spell of Shakespeare and Edmund Kean, that " romance lives but in books. The goblin is driven from the hearth, and the rainbow is robbed of its mystery "; or ask " who would live in a region of Mists, Game Laws, Indemnity Bills, &c., when there is such a place as Italy ? " But in his last illness he wanted Cobbett to be elected to Parliament, said : " O that I had two double plumpers for him." When he heard that Cobbett had been attacking the Kentucky settlement where his brother and sister-in-law were, he was "all at elbows" to hear from them the truth of it. He wanted to put his mite on the Liberal side before he died. For he regarded the Liberals as working to destroy that "superstition against all innovation and improvement" which was begotten by fear of the Revolution. The soldiers appeared to him to be "cheated into an *esprit de corps* by a red coat, a band, and colours"; parsons appeared as lambs in drawing-rooms, lions in vestrys—hypocrites to believers, cowards to unbelievers, and he trusted that as the ancients had some animals unknown to us, so posterity would miss "the black badger with tricornered hat." Much though he loved scenery, human nature was finer in his eyes, and "the sward richer for the tread of a real nervous English foot." In the same way, he knew that his thoughts and his poems took a deeper tone from all human experience, knew, as Endymion said,

> "the war, the deeds,
> The disappointment, the anxiety,
> Imagination's struggles far and nigh,
> All human; bearing in themselves this good,
> That they are still the air, the subtle food,
> To make us feel existence. . . ."

Plainly too, though he longed for an age so sheltered from annoy that he should never know how change the moons, he had a profound feeling for the history and evolution of his own planet. It is shown in the sonnet on Ailsa Craig and its two dead eternities,

"The last in air, the former in the deep,"

and in the speech of Oceanus, in "Hyperion," when he asks the Titans to be comforted, because they fall

" By course of Nature's law, not force
Of thunder, or of Jove . . ."

because

"On our heels a fresh perfection treads,
A power more strong in beauty, born of us
And fated to excel us, as we pass
In glory that old Darkness."

To his character, conduct, and appearance there were the same two sides as to his thought. He could enjoy the sensation "about three degrees on this side of faintness" as he lay in bed at eleven—" if I had teeth of pearl and the breath of lilies I should call it languor, but as I am I must call it laziness "— the sensation which brought forth the ode on Indolence ; but he could fight a butcher for torturing a cat, and beat him. If he could be hurt by a review, he would not have avoided a duel with the scholar, gentleman, and blackguard, that wrote it ; and he felt no humility towards anything but the Eternal Being, the Principle of Beauty, and the Memory of Great Men. The refuge of humour also was his. Some of his letters break into a playfulness like Lamb's, as when he asks his brother and sister-in-law if in Kentucky they got any spirits—" now you might easily distil some whisky—and going into the woods, set up a whisky-shop for the monkeys . . . ; " and bids the girl " sew *off* " her husband's buttons ; and having copied out for them " La belle Dame sans Merci," jests about " with kisses four " which used to end the stanza :

> " She took me to her elfin grot,
> And there she gaz'd and sighed deep,
> And there I shut her wild sad eyes—
> So kissed to sleep . . ."

or when after praising claret as his only " palate passion," he puts in that he was forgetting game— " I must plead guilty to the breast of a partridge, the back of a hare, the backbone of a grouse, the wing and side of a pheasant, and a woodcock *passim.*" Whatever is lacking it is seldom ease or gusto. Of all famous letters Keats's are excelled by none in their direct presentation of the moment's phases of mind and moods of temperament ; by reason of their closeness to those variations they are sometimes as difficult as they are pleasant to follow, with their shadowy memorials of the hazel eyes that flashed, the cheek that glowed, the mouth that shook, for love of what was noble and beautiful, for hatred of the mean or crass or false—of the look as of an eagle, a deer, a delphic priestess.

One of the moods altogether free from languor and softness, in the letters, is that swift pugnacity of his boyhood, mingled with a baser touchiness about his birth and his five feet of height. His guardian was the only man in England, he said, who would dare to say a thing to him which he did not approve of, without its being resented or noticed. Disliking a reputation as disciple of Hunt, and touchily fearing influence, he refused to visit Shelley; he did not care if they were hurt, and, if they were going to dissect and anatomise him, "Who's afraid? Aye! Tom! Demme if I am." Apparently because he invented a tinge of *hauteur* in Shelley's letter he rejected with pepper the invitation to join him in Italy. Independent he would be, in "Endymion" without judgment, as he himself admitted; but thereafter independent perhaps with judgment.

His contempt for public opinion, as for that most vulgar of all crowds, the literary, was acute. Were his nights' labours to be burnt unseen every morning he believed that he would write "from the mere yearning and fondness" he had for the beautiful; and he had seldom any doubt of his powers for poetry; his heart distended "with pride and obstinacy" as he thought of what his diligence "might in time probably effect." That his reputation was bad after "Endymion," he well knew, and he could not forget it; but said he,

"Whenever I find myself growing vapourish, I rouse myself, wash, and put on a clean shirt, brush my hair and clothes, tie my shoestrings neatly, and in fact adonize as if I were going out. Then, all clean and comfortable, I sit down to write."

His fine, compact, small body, was one to look well under such treatment.

His "thirst for glory" must have quieted after 1817. Thoughts of taking to journalism, even to Tea-brokerage with his guardian, of going on an Indiaman as surgeon, tempted him a little in 1819, but he kept to poetry. He grew older. A foreboding that his discipline was to come, "and plenty of it too," without being sought for, occurred to him. And he hoped that he had become more of a philosopher—more often contented to read and think— less of

"A pet lamb in a sentimental farce."

It was thought that he had lost the "poetical ardour and fire he once had" : his relish for scenery and the talk at Hunt's or Haydon's was gone. The hour of "splendour in the grass, of glory in the flower" had, he knew, passed away. He was moulting and losing his feathers and wings, hoping for "patient sublunary legs" in place of them. Poetry, love, and consumption broke down an incalculable development. Even the odes, "Hyperion," and "Lamia" cannot be said to mark full harmony attained between the poet's intellect, his manly grasp of life, and his "morbidity" or sensitiveness of temperament.

The story of the end need be retold but briefly. The "Charmian" who haunted him in September, 1818, and the "new strange and threatening sorrow" then approaching, were dismissed by poetry. Poetry,

CHARACTER

that woman, and his brother's dying sickness, together with the nervousness of poor health, a sore throat, and doses of mercury, had destroyed his "self-possession and magnanimity," at least until "poetry conquered." About a month later he met Fanny Brawne, a girl of eighteen, at Dilke's house. He was at once her "vassal" but could describe her critically to his brother and sister-in-law—how "her Profile is better than her full face which indeed is not full but pale and thin without showing any bone "— her " Arms good, her hands bad-ish—her feet tolerable "—" ignorant—monstrous in her behaviour, flying out in all directions, calling people such names —that I was forced lately to make use of the term *Minx*—this is I think not from any innate vice but from a penchant she has for acting stylishly." She was to conquer Poetry. She accepted his adoration, and returned it apparently without giving more than the slightest pretext for doubt or jealousy. For a time, because he was then in the midst of his greatest period, and had to find vent for the pressure of poetry within him, Keats continued to work at "Hyperion," "The Eve of St. Agnes," and "Isabella," and wrote "Lamia," "Otho the Great," and his finest short poems. To do this he had to live away from Fanny Brawne, at Shanklin and Winchester: had he been near her long, at this time, love and poetry together, not to speak of the "hateful literary chit-chat" of Hampstead, would have been insupportable. When he wrote verses directly to her he proved it: of his best qualities hardly anything survived; he painted love and jealousy, frantically, piteously, except once when he foretasted death, if he did not see truly beyond it:

> "This living hand, now warm and capable
> Of earnest grasping, would, if it were cold
> And in the icy silence of the tomb,
> So haunt thy days and chill thy dreaming nights
> That thou wouldst wish thy own heart dry of blood
> So in my veins red life might stream again,
> And thou be conscience-calmed—see here it is—
> I hold it towards you."

It is finer than anything in his play, "Otho the Great."

Thus "plunged deeply in imaginary interests," Keats worked and wrote letters to Fanny Brawne which he had sometimes to cut short lest he should be "uncrystallized and dissolved" by the intercourse; for if he began with the dream of dismissing her by that means from his mind, he ended by exclaiming that his creed was love, and she its only tenet: "My love is selfish. I cannot breathe without you." Love was breaking his spirit. He told her that if she loved another he would still love her—"but what hatred shall I have for another": that he ached to be with her and would die for one hour—" for what is in the world ? " All that he could bring her, he said, was " a swooning admiration of her beauty." He returned to London, caught cold again, had a violent rush of blood to his lungs, and lay too ill to see her for more than a few seconds daily. The thought that she was "a little inclined to the Cressid," his greedy adoration—"ever and ever and without reserve"—impatience of the barrier built by sickness between them, the belief that he was to leave no immortal work behind him, the "irritability and general weakness" proceeding from his anxieties, and "the too great excitement of poetry," all exhausted him. "I appeal to you," he cried in July 1820, "by the blood of that Christ you believe in : Do not write to me if you have done anything this month which it would have pained me to have seen." The air of a room "empty" of Fanny Brawne seemed to him unhealthy for him to breathe : he felt, therefore, that he could not recover in Italy. At thought of the separation he wished to die; he sickened at imagination of the every-day world casting eyes on her; he hated men and women. He seldom thought now of his brother and sister-in-law. On the ship in September Fanny Brawne's phrases rang in his ears, and eternally he saw her figure eternally vanishing. Yet off Dorset, after a day on the rocky shore, he wrote the sonnet, "Bright star, would I were steadfast as thou art," opposite "A Lover's Complaint" in his copy of Shakespeare's poems. At Naples, her keepsakes went through him "like a spear," the silk lining put by her in his travelling cap scaided his head. If he had had any chance of recovery, he said, the passion would have killed him. He was no longer "a citizen of the world." His spirit loathed the sentinels on the opera stage at Naples, "the continual visible tyranny of this government," and he dreaded to leave his bones "in the midst of this despotism." Had it not been entrusted to Severn, he would have poisoned himself with the laudanum he had brought with him. He lingered on at Rome, punning, bleeding, raving, feeling the flowers growing over him, in that "posthumous life," until he thanked God for death on 23rd February 1821.

BIBLIOGRAPHY

Poetical Works of Keats. Edited by H. Buxton Forman. Oxford University Press.

Works and Letters of John Keats. Edited by H. Buxton Forman. Gowans and Gray.

Poems of Keats. Edited by Ernest de Sélincourt. Methuen.

Keats. By Sidney Colvin. Macmillan & Co.

Oxford Lectures on Poetry. By A. C. Bradley. Macmillan and Co.

Studies in Poetry. By Stopford Brooke. Duckworth & Co.

Studies and Essays. By Mary Suddard. Cambridge University Press.

Lord Byron and Some of his Contemporaries. By Leigh Hunt.

The Autobiography of Leigh Hunt, with Reminiscences of Friends and Contemporaries.

Letters of Shelley. Edited by Roger Ingpen. Pitmans.

Life of Benjamin Robert Haydon. Edited and compiled by Tom Taylor.

Benjamin Robert Haydon: Correspondence and Table Talk. With memoir by F. W. Haydon.

The Fancy. By John Hamilton Reynolds. Edited by John Masefield. Elkin Mathews.

Poems of Leigh Hunt.

INDEX

ABBEY, Richard, 9
Anatomy of Melancholy. See Burton
Arnold, Matthew, 65

BAILEY, Benjamin, 30
Beattie, 11
Beaumont and Fletcher, 15
Bedhampton, 17, 29
Bradley, A. C., 31, 73
Brawne, Fanny, 21, 30, 32, 48, 61, 70-72, 76, 77, 87, *et seq.*
Brooke, Stopford, 78
Brown, Charles Armitage, 28, 29, 70
Burford Bridge, 17, 40
Burton, Robert, 16, 32
Byron, 9, 10, 16, 25, 65

CARISBROOKE, 12, 17, 40
Chapman, 11, 35, 37
"Charmian." See Charlotte Cox
Chatterton, 16, 30, 60
Chaucer, 13, 15, 16
Chichester, 17, 29
"Christabel." See Coleridge
Clarke, Charles Cowden, 8, 9, 11
Cobbett, William, 10, 81, 82
Coleridge, 30, 60
Cox, Charlotte, 31, 86
Crabbe, George, 16

DANTE, 13, 16
Dilke, Charles Wentworth, 28, 29, 87

"Don Juan." See Byron
Dryden, 58

ELGIN Marbles, 25, 35, 37, 43

FRENCH Revolution, 7, 82

HAMPSTEAD, 48, 69, 87
Haydon, B. R., 13, 25, 86
Hazlitt, W., 13, 15, 16, 30
Hunt, Leigh, 9, 10, 13, 16, 21, 23-25, 30, 85, 86

ITALY, 89

KEAN, Edmund, 18
Keats, Fanny, 21, 31
— George, 9, 21, 22, 75
— Georgiana (*née* Wylie), 22, 31
— John, birth, 7; parentage, 7, 8; at school, 8; brothers, 21, 22; begins to write, 9, 11; apprenticed, 9; walking hospitals, 10; travels, 17-18, 19, 37, 38; his reading, 11, 13, 14, 16, 35; love of England, 16, 17; illness, 17; his "Poems," 34, *et seq.*, 40; his "Endymion," 40, *et seq.*; his "Lamia," &c., 48, *et seq.*; last illness and death, 88-90; character, 11, 50, 74, *et seq.*; in relation to women, 21, 30, 31, 32, 33, 46; friends, see under Haydon, Leigh

INDEX

Hunt, &c.; interests, 10, 81; letters, 84; quoted, 18, 20, 21, 22, 26, 30, 31, 38, 74, *et seq.*; manuscripts, 29

Poems

"A Song of Opposites," 55
"Bright star, would I were steadfast as thou art," 71, 89
"Cap and Bells," 29, 59, 60, 70
"Endymion," 19, 23, 30, 33, *et seq.*, 48, 51, 53, 59, 61, 62, 70, 80, 82, 85
Epistle to George Keats, 37, 80-81
Epistle to J. H. Reynolds, 26
"Fame, like a wayward girl, will still be coy," 58
"Hence Burgundy, Claret, and Port," 26
"Hyperion," 19, 20, 29, 48, 61, *et seq.*, 76, 83, 86, 87; Second Version, 68, *et seq.*
"I had a dove and the sweet dove died," 37
"Isabella," 26, 48-49, 50, 51, 52, 58, 79, 81
"I stood tiptoe upon a little hill," 40
"La Belle Dame sans Merci," 48, 52, 59, 72, 84
"Lamia," 44, 58-59, 61, 80, 87
"Lines on the Mermaid Tavern," 28, 51, 72
"Meg Merrilies," 48
"O blush not so! O blush not so!" 26
Odes, 51, 52, 72, 86
Ode on a Grecian Urn, 56-57, 72, 77
Ode on Indolence, 57, 76, 83
Ode on Melancholy, 53, 54, 57, 76
Ode to a Nightingale, 29, 54, 55, 56, 72, 76
Ode to Psyche, 52-53

"On first looking into Chapman's Homer," 12
"On leaving some friends at an early hour," 36
"On seeing the Elgin Marbles," 35, 37, 43
"O sorrow, sorrow, why dost borrow?" 59
"Otho the Great," 61, 66, 68, 77, 87, 88
"Robin Hood," 27, 28, 51, 59
"Sleep and Poetry," 20, 79
"Spenserean stanzas on C. A. Brown," 29
"The Eve of St. Agnes," 51, 52, 59, 61, 63, 65, 72, 77, 87
"The Eve of St. Mark," 59-60, 65
"This living hand, now warm and capable," 88
"To Ailsa Craig," 18, 83
"To a lady seen for a few moments at Vauxhall," 31
"To Autumn," 51, 53
"To Fancy," 50
"To Haydon," 25
"To Leigh Hunt," 23
"Unfelt, unheard, unseen," 32
"What the thrush said," 51
"When I have fears that I may cease to be," 26
"Where's the Poet? show him! show him!" 76
Keats, Tom, 9, 21, 22, 48, 85
"King Lear." See Shakespeare

LAMB, Charles, 25, 83

MARGATE, 17
Milton, 14, 15, 16, 40, 43, 57, 62, 63, 76
Moore, Thomas, 15, 16, 24, 43

OXFORD, 17, 30

INDEX

"PARADISE Lost." See Milton
"Peter Bell the Third." See Shelley
Pindar, 55
Polwhele, 11
Pope, 36
Pre-Raphaelites, 60

Quarterly Review, 48

REGENT, the Prince, 7, 23
Reynolds, John Hamilton, 14, 21, 25-28, 74
— the Misses, 30
Rice, James, 28
Rogers, Samuel, 3, 16

SEVERN, Joseph, 30, 90
Shakespeare, 14, 39, 41, 43, 58, 75, 77, 81, 89

Shanklin, 17, 29, 87
Shelley, 10, 21, 30, 46, 55, 70, 78, 85
Smith, Horace, 30
Southey, 16
Spenser, 9, 40, 57
Suddard, Mary, 54

TEIGNMOUTH, 17
Tighe, Mrs., 11
Titian, 43
Trelawney, Edward, 29

WELLS, Charles, 30
Westminster, 61
Winchester, 17, 60, 71, 89
"Witch of Atlas." See Shelley
Woodhouse, R., 29
Wordsworth, 7, 13, 14, 16, 25, 29, 30, 40, 46, 78
Wylie, Georgiana. See Keats

THE PEOPLE'S BOOKS

General Editor—H. C. O'NEILL

"With the 'People's Books' in hand there should be nobody of average intelligence unable to secure self-education."—*Sunday Times.*

NOW READY (October 1914)
THE FIRST 108 VOLUMES

1. The Foundations of Science . . . By W.C.D.Whetham,M.A.,F.R.S.
2. Embryology—The Beginnings of Life By Prof. Gerald Leighton, M.D.
3. Biology . . . . By Prof. W. D. Henderson, M.A.
4. Zoology: The Study of Animal Life { By Prof. E. W. MacBride, M.A., F.R.S.
5. Botany; The Modern Study of Plants { By M. C. Stopes, D.Sc., Ph.D., F.L.S.
6. Bacteriology . . . . . . By W. E. Carnegie Dickson, M.D.
7. The Structure of the Earth . . By Prof. T. G. Bonney, F.R.S.
8. Evolution . . . . By E. S. Goodrich, M.A., F.R.S.
10. Heredity . . . . By J. A. S. Watson, B.Sc.
11. Inorganic Chemistry . . . By Prof. E. C. C. Baly, F.R.S.
12. Organic Chemistry . . . . By Prof. J. B. Cohen, B.Sc., F.R.S.
13. The Principles of Electricity . . By Norman R. Campbell, M.A.
14. Radiation . . . . By P. Phillips, D.Sc.
15. The Science of the Stars . . . By E.W. Maunder, F.R.A.S.
16. The Science of Light . . . . By P. Phillips, D.Sc.
17. Weather Science . . . . . By R. G. K. Lempfert, M.A.
18. Hypnotism and Self-Education . . By A. M. Hutchison, M.D.
19. The Baby: A Mother's Book . . By a University Woman.
20. Youth and Sex—Dangers and Safe- } By Mary Scharlieb,M.D., M.S., and guards for Boys and Girls . . } F. Arthur Sibly, M.A., LL.D.
21. Marriage and Motherhood . . . { By H. S. Davidson, M.B., F.R.C.S.E.
22. Lord Kelvin . . . . . . By A. Russell,M.A.,D.Sc.,M.I.E.E.
23. Huxley . . . . By Professor G. Leighton, M.D.
24. Sir William Huggins and Spectro- } By E.W. Maunder, F.R.A.S.,of the scopic Astronomy . . . . } Royal Observatory, Greenwich.
26. Henri Bergson . . . . . By H. Wildon Carr, Litt.D.
27. Psychology . . . . . . By H. J. Watt, M.A., Ph.D., D.Phil.
28. Ethics . . . . By Canon Rashdall, D.Litt., F.B.A.
29. Kant's Philosophy . . . . { By A. D. Lindsay, M.A., of Balliol College, Oxford.
32. Roman Catholicism . . . { By H. B. Coxon. Preface, Mgr. R. H. Benson.
33. The Oxford Movement . . . By Wilfrid Ward.
34. The Bible and Criticism . . . { By W. H. Bennett, D.D., Litt.D., and W. F. Adeney, D.D.
36. The Growth of Freedom . . . By H. W. Nevinson.
37. Bismarck and the Origin of the } Professor F. M. Powicke. German Empire . . . . }
38. Oliver Cromwell . . . . . By Hilda Johnstone, M.A.
39. Mary Queen of Scots . . . By E. O'Neill, M.A.
40. Cecil John Rhodes, 1853-1902 . . By Ian D. Colvin.
41. Julius Caesar . . . . . . By Hilary Hardinge.
42. England in the Making . . . { By Prof. F. J. C. Hearnshaw, M.A., LL.D.
43. England in the Middle Ages . . By E. O'Neill, M.A.
44. The Monarchy and the People . . By W. T. Waugh, M.A.
45. The Industrial Revolution . . . By Arthur Jones, M.A.
46. Empire and Democracy . . . By G. S. Veitch, M.A., Litt.D.
47. Women's Suffrage . . . . . By M. G. Fawcett, LL.D.
51. Shakespeare . . . . . . By Prof. C. H. Herford, Litt.D.
52. Wordsworth . . . . . . By Rosaline Masson.
53. Pure Gold—A Choice of Lyrics and } By H. C. O'Neill. Sonnets . . . . }
54. Francis Bacon . . . . . By Prof. A. R. Skemp, M.A.
55. The Brontës . . . . . . By Flora Masson.

THE PEOPLE'S BOOKS—(continued)

56. Carlyle . . . . By L. MacLean Watt.
57. Dante . . . . By A. G. Ferrers Howell.
59. Common Faults in Writing English . By Henry Alexander, B.A.
60. A Dictionary of Synonyms . . . By Austin K. Gray, B.A.
61. Home Rule . . . . . . { By L. G. Redmond Howard. Preface by Robert Harcourt, M.P.
62. Practical Astronomy . . . . By H. Macpherson, Jr., F.R.A.S.
63. Aviation . . . . By Sydney F. Walker, R.N.
64. Navigation . . . . . . By William Hall, R.N., B.A.
65. Pond Life . . . . . . By E. C. Ash, M.R.A.C.
66. Dietetics . . . . By Alex. Bryce, M.D., D.P.H.
67. Aristotle . . . . By Prof. A. E. Taylor, M.A., F.B.A.
68. Friedrich Nietzsche . . . . By M. A. Mügge,
69. Eucken: A Philosophy of Life . . By A. J. Jones, M.A., B.Sc., Ph.D.
70. The Experimental Psychology of Beauty . . . . } By C. W. Valentine, B.A., D.Phil.
71. The Problem of Truth . . . . By H. Wildon Carr, Litt.D.
72. The Church of England . . . By Rev. Canon Masterman.
73. Anglo-Catholicism . . . . . By A. E. Manning Foster.
74. The Free Churches . . . . By Rev. Edward Shillito, M.A.
75. Judaism . . . . By Ephraim Levine, M.A.
76. Theosophy . . . . . . By Annie Besant.
78. Wellington and Waterloo . . . By Major G. W. Redway.
79. Mediaeval Socialism . . . . By Bede Jarrett, O.P., M.A.
80. Syndicalism . . . . . . By J. H. Harley, M.A.
82. Co-operation . . . . . . By Joseph Clayton.
83. Insurance as a Means of Investment By W. A. Robertson, F.F.A.
85. A History of English Literature . By A. Compton-Rickett, LL.D.
87. Charles Lamb . . . . . . By Flora Masson.
88. Goethe . . . . By Prof. C. H. Herford, Litt.D.
92. The Training of the Child . . . By G. Spiller.
93. Tennyson . . . . By Aaron Watson.
94. The Nature of Mathematics . . By P. E. B. Jourdain, M.A.
95. Applications of Electricity . . . By Alex. Ogilvie, B.Sc.
96. Gardening . . . . . . By A. Cecil Bartlett.
98. Atlas of the World . . . . By J. Bartholomew, F.R.G.S.
100. History of Greece . . . . . By E. Fearenside, M.A.
101. Luther and the Reformation . . By Leonard D. Agate, M.A.
103. Turkey and the Eastern Question . By John Macdonald, M.A.
104. Architecture . . . . . . By Mrs. Arthur Bell.
105. Trade Unions . . . . . . By Joseph Clayton.
106. Everyday Law . . . . . By J. J. Adams.
107. R. L. Stevenson . . . . . By Rosaline Masson.
108. Shelley . . . . By Sydney Waterlow, M.A.
110. British Birds . . . . . . By F. B. Kirkman, B.A.
111. Spiritualism . . . . . . By J. Arthur Hill.
112. Kindergarten Teaching at Home . { By Two Members of the National Froebel Union.
113. Schopenhauer . . . . . . By Margrieta Beer, M.A.
114. The Stock Exchange . . . . By J. F. Wheeler.
115. Coleridge . . . . By S. L. Bensusan.
116. The Crusades . . . . . . By M. M. C. Calthrop.
117. Wild Flowers . . . . . . By Macgregor Skene, B.Sc.
118. Principles of Logic . . . . By Stanley Williams, B.A.
119. The Foundations of Religion . . By Stanley A. Cook, M.A.
120. History of Rome . . . . . By A. F. Giles, M.A.
121. Land, Industry, and Taxation . . By Frederick Verinder.
122. Canada . . . . By Ford Fairford.
123. Tolstoy . . . . By L. Winstanley, M.A.
124. Greek Literature . . . . . By H. J. W. Tillyard, M.A.
125. The Navy of To-Day . . . . By Percival Hislam.
126. Keats . . . . By Edward Thomas.
127. Roman Civilization . . . . By A. F. Giles, M.A.
128. French Self-Tutor . . . . . By W. M. Conacher.

LONDON AND EDINBURGH: T. C. & E. C. JACK
NEW YORK: DODGE PUBLISHING CO.

FURTHER READING

By Edward Thomas

The Childhood of Edward Thomas, a fragment of autobiography. Faber 1938.
Feminine Influence on the Poets. Martin Secker 1910. (Keats & Fanny Brawne).
Maurice Maeterlinck. Methuen 1911.
Walter Pater, A Critical Study. Martin Secker 1913. (Important on development of style).
A Literary Pilgrim in England. Methuen 1917.
Collected Poems. Faber. Always in print.

Other Titles:

Eleanor Farjeon: *Edward Thomas, The Last Four Years.* OUP 1958 and Alan Sutton 1998.
Edna Longley, ed: *A Language Not To Be Betrayed. Selected Prose of Edward Thomas.* Carcanet Press 1981.
Professor R. George Thomas: *Edward Thomas, A Portrait.* OUP 1985.

All these books can be found in the Dymock Poets Archive and Study Centre at the Cheltenham & Gloucester College of Higher Education.